P·E·R·F·E·C·T
ITALIAN
COUNTRY COOKING

D1372402

P·E·R·F·E·C·T
ITALIAN
COUNTRY COOKING

DORLING KINDERSLEY
LONDON • NEW YORK • STUTTGART • MOSCOW

A DORLING KINDERSLEY BOOK

Created and Produced by
CARROLL & BROWN LIMITED
5 Lonsdale Road
London NW6 6RA

Editorial Director Jeni Wright
Editors Norma MacMillan
Anna Brandenburger
Editorial Assistant Julia Alcock

Art Editor Vicky Zentner
Designers Lucy De Rosa
Alan Watt
Production Editor Wendy Rogers

First published in Great Britain in 1997
by Dorling Kindersley Limited
9 Henrietta Street, London WC2E 8PS

Previously published in 1993 under the title
Look & Cook Italian Country Cooking.

Copyright © 1993, 1997 Dorling Kindersley Limited
Text copyright © 1993, 1997 Anne Willan Inc.

Visit us on the World Wide Web at http://www.dk.com

All rights reserved. No part of this publication may be
reproduced, stored in a retrieval system, or transmitted in
any form or by any means, electronic, mechanical, photocopying,
recording, or otherwise, without the prior written permission
of the copyright owner.

A CIP catalogue record for this book is available
from the British Library

ISBN 0-7513-0385-2

Reproduced by Colourscan, Singapore
Printed and bound in Singapore by Star Standard

CONTENTS

PERFECT ITALIAN COUNTRY COOKING

Welcome to **Perfect Italian Country Cooking**. This volume is designed to be the simplest, most informative cookbook you'll ever own. It is the closest I can come to sharing my personal techniques for cooking my favourite recipes without actually being with you in the kitchen.

EQUIPMENT

Equipment and ingredients often determine whether or not you can cook a particular dish, so **Perfect Italian Country Cooking** illustrates everything you need at the beginning of each recipe. You'll see at a glance how long a recipe takes to cook, how many servings it makes, what the finished dish looks like, and how much preparation can be done ahead. When you start to cook, you will find that the preparation and cooking are organized into easy-to-follow steps.

INGREDIENTS

Each stage has its own colour coding, and everything is shown in photographs with brief text accompanying each step. You will never be in doubt as to what it is you are doing, why you are doing it, or how it should look.

🍽 SERVES 4–6 ⏱ WORK TIME 25–35 MINUTES 🍲 COOKING TIME 20–30 MINUTES

I've also included helpful hints and ideas under "Anne Says". These may list an alternative ingredient or piece of equipment, or explain the reason for using a certain method, or offer advice on mastering a particular technique. Similarly, if there is a crucial stage in a recipe when things can go wrong, I've included some warnings called "Take Care".

Many of the photographs are annotated to pinpoint why a certain piece of equipment works best, or how food should look at that stage of cooking. Because presentation is so important, there is a picture of the finished dish at the end of each recipe, often with serving suggestions.

Thanks to all this information, you can't go wrong. I'll be with you every step of the way. So please come with me into the kitchen to look, cook, and create some delicious recipes from **Perfect Italian Country Cooking**.

WHY ITALIAN COUNTRY COOKING?

The Italians I know look to the countryside for the authentic food of the people. They never think in terms of a national cuisine, but rather in terms of Italy's provinces, each of which has developed its own distinctive cooking style and traditions.

Simplicity is a common theme. The cook uses just a few techniques to feed the family on a daily basis. Kitchens are devoid of gadgets, and standard utensils are kept to a minimum. Until after World War II, even ovens were a luxury in the country kitchen. Roasting was done on the hearth, and bread baking was a once-weekly event in the communal oven. Until very recently, a housewife was taught to cook by her mother and her grandmother, carrying their recipes in her head. If she were lucky, there would be an heirloom notebook of family favourites to serve as an aide mémoire.

Though apparently limited by equipment, technique, and repertoire, the Italian cook is blessed with the greatest gift of all: fine ingredients. Seasonal foods at their peak of flavour form the cornerstone of Italian country cooking. Cooks set out to make the most of what they have, and taste is the prime concern. The humble carrot bursts with flavour when it is simmered until meltingly soft. The much-used method of simmering meats partially covered with liquid ensures they do not dry out during lengthy cooking, while distinct flavours meld in the process. The popular agrodolce, or sweet-sour, combinations emphasize balance rather than contrast. If the dish turns out to be a visual knockout too, so much the better, but don't expect elaborate presentations and garnishes in the Italian countryside.

The traditional menu is composed of a succession of modest courses adding up to a substantial meal. A primo piatto, or first course, of polenta, pasta, or risotto is followed, after a suitable interval, by the secondo piatto of fish, poultry, or meat, with vegetables or salad. Fruit and/or cheese usually brings the meal to a close. Desserts tend to be reserved for special occasions, such as birthdays and Christmas, as does the antipasto, a light dish served before the main meal, or pasto.

However, the whole style of eating is changing. The main meal always used to be served at mid-day, but modern schedules make such timing impractical, especially in big cities, so that dinner has become more important. At the same time, with the move towards lighter eating, what was once the primo piatto now often becomes the entire meal.

What has not changed, and surely never will, is the Italian passion for good food. Nearly everyone you meet in Italy is an authority, quoting a guiding genius who presides over the family kitchen. It is a spirit that can be translated into any language and can flourish anywhere in the world. It is the essence of Italian country cooking – a respect for good ingredients and a desire to make the most of them in the simplest way possible.

RECIPE CHOICE

An Italian cook tries to plan a meal around the produce available in the local market, and I like to do the same. Hearty meals stave off the winter cold and lighter ones welcome a warm spring day. Summer is the time to choose recipes abundant in fresh vegetables and aromatic herbs. Below is a summary of recipes you will find in this volume.

ANTIPASTI AND PRIMI PIATTI

Roman-Style Artichokes with Herbs and Garlic (Carciofi alla Romana): in an unusual presentation, young artichokes are stuffed with parsley, mint, and garlic, then braised and served with their stalks pointing upwards. *Slow-Braised Artichoke Hearts (Carciofi in Umido)*: here artichokes are cut into wedges, then cooked with the same herbs, for a different result. *Grilled Mussels with Red Pepper Topping (Cozze Gratinate)*: salty-tasting mussels are steamed, topped with chopped roasted red pepper, parsley, garlic, and breadcrumbs, then grilled. *Grilled Clams (Vongole Gratinate)*: succulent clams are covered with the same savoury topping as the mussels. *Grilled Mussels with Parsley and Capers (Cozze al Prezzemolo e Capperi)*: parsley, capers, garlic, and breadcrumbs highlight the delicate flavour of mussels. *Baked Polenta with Wild Mushrooms and Fontina (Polenta Pasticciata)*: meaty wild mushrooms are simmered in white wine and stock, then baked with layers of polenta and fontina cheese. *Baked Polenta with Parma Ham and Eggs (Polenta Pasticciata con Prosciutto e Uova)*: ham and eggs are baked within polenta layers. *Straw and Hay Pasta with Cream, Ham, and Mushrooms (Paglia e Fieno alla Ghiottona)*: homemade white and green fettuccine is embellished with ham, mushrooms, and peas in a rich cream sauce. *Noodles with Sage and Butter (Tonnarelli al Salvia e Burro)*: fresh sage and butter complement plain and spinach noodles. *Prawn Risotto (Risotto ai Gamberi)*: creamy white rice and pink prawns make an elegant first course. *Asparagus Risotto (Risotto con gli Asparagi)*: spring is the season to cook asparagus risotto. *Quills with Spicy Tomato and Bacon Sauce (Penne all'Arrabbiata)*: quill-shaped pasta is tossed in a lively tomato sauce with chilli, crisp bacon, and mushrooms. *Spaghetti with Tomato and Chilli Sauce (Spaghetti alla Satana)*: an even spicier tomato sauce coats spaghetti. *Baked Rigatoni with Meatballs (Timballo di Rigatoni)*: tiny meatballs flavoured with Parmesan are hidden between layers of pasta and tomato sauce – hearty enough for a complete meal. *Baked Ziti with*

Mozzarella and Olives (Timballo di Ziti con Mozzarella e Olive): mozzarella cheese, black olives, and tomato sauce flavoured with anchovies lend a Mediterranean taste to baked ziti. *Fresh Polenta with Vegetable Stew (Polenta con Fricandò)*: a selection of vegetables is served on a bed of polenta. *Barbecued Polenta with Vegetable Stew (Quadrati di Polenta con Fricandò)*: a similar vegetable stew is served with barbecued polenta squares. *Spinach and Potato Gnocchi in Tomato-Cream Sauce (Gnocchi Verdi al Sugo di Pomodoro e Panna)*: tomato-cream sauce complements little potato dumplings flavoured with spinach. *Spinach and Potato Gnocchi with Cheese (Gnocchi Verdi alla Bava)*: the lightness of potato gnocchi can be fully appreciated in this simple dish served with melted cheese. *Plain Gnocchi with Gorgonzola Sauce (Gnocchi al Gorgonzola)*: blue-veined Gorgonzola, fresh thyme, and cream form the sauce for these plain gnocchi.

SECONDI PIATTI

Sole Fillets Marinated in Wine Vinegar (Sfogi in Saor): in this traditional Venetian dish, strips of sole are pan-fried, then marinated in a sweet-sour mixture of onion, red wine vinegar, and raisins, with pine nuts. *Sole Fillets Marinated with Wine Vinegar and Saffron (Pesce a Scapece)*: saffron lends a golden hue to the sole. *Beef Braised in Red Wine (Stufato di Manzo al Barbera)*: a speciality of northern Italy; beef is browned in olive oil, then cooked in the oven in red wine and beef stock.

Braised Lamb with Potatoes and Tomatoes (Agnello al Forno con Patate e Pomodori): in this classic dish from the South, lamb is braised in the oven with white wine, tomatoes, and potatoes. *Milanese Veal Escalopes (Scaloppine alla Milanese)*: veal escalopes at their simple best, coated with Parmesan and breadcrumbs, then sautéed in butter and olive oil, and garnished with lemon slices. *Veal Escalopes with Parma Ham (Scaloppine alla Modenese)*: a similar preparation adds Parma ham and fontina or Gruyère cheese. *Sautéed Liver and Onions (Fegato alla Veneziana)*: onions are cooked until meltingly soft, then combined with thin slices of sautéed calf's liver in this Venetian classic. *Sautéed Liver with Wine Vinegar (Fegato all'Aceto):* red wine vinegar and parsley complement quickly sautéed liver. *Devilled Chicken (Pollo alla Diavola):* a zesty marinade of lemon juice, olive oil, and chilli flavours and tenderizes chicken before grilling. *Grilled Chicken Drumsticks with Rosemary (Gambe di Pollo ai Ferri):* easy-to-handle chicken drumsticks are marinated in garlic and rosemary – ideal for a picnic. *Spinach-Stuffed Veal Rolls (Messicani di Vitello):* veal escalopes rolled around a stuffing of spinach, Parmesan, and walnuts are served with their cooking liquid. *Roast Loin of Pork with Garlic and Rosemary (Arista):* simple but superb. *Braised Pork with Madeira Sauce (Arrosto di Maiale in Casseruola):* the pork is braised with onions, and served with carrot batons. *Hunter's Chicken (Pollo alla Cacciatora):* in this international favourite, chicken is flavoured with white wine, garlic, and rosemary, and served with sautéed escarole. *Hunter's Chicken with Black Olives (Pollo alla Cacciatora con le Olive):* black olives, anchovies, and red wine vinegar add punch to sautéed chicken, while chicory replaces escarole.

DOLCI

Strawberry and Raspberry Hazelnut Tart (Crostata di Fragole e Lamponi): delicate hazelnut pastry, Marsala-flavoured whipped cream, and red berries are the perfect conclusion to a special occasion. *Strawberry Tart with Chocolate Cream (Crostata di Fragole al Cioccolato):* a chocolate lover's dream! *Ricotta Cheesecake (Crostata di Ricotta):* creamy ricotta cheese forms the background for crunchy almonds, sultanas, orange zest, and candied orange peel. *Chocolate Ricotta Pie (Crostata di Ricotta al Cioccolato):* chopped chocolate and orange zest mixed with ricotta fill this rectangular pie – ideal for cutting bite-sized portions. *Walnut Cake with Caramel Topping (Torta di Noci):* no flour is to be found in this rich, buttery cake. *Walnut Cake with Raisins (Torta di Noci e Uve Passe):* this is studded with grappa-soaked raisins – the ultimate temptation. *Grapefruit Granita (Granita di Pompelmo):* frozen grapefruit juice is a refreshing finale to any meal, and can be served with All Souls' Day almond biscuits. *Coffee Granita (Granita di Caffè):* rosettes of Amaretto-flavoured whipped cream decorate this frozen dessert. *Apple Cake (Torta di Mele):* this delicious, moist cake is topped with apple slices, then glazed. *Pear Cake (Torta di Pere):* caramelized pears replace the apples in this simple variation. *Whipped Cream Cake with Chocolate and Nuts (Zuccotto Toscano):* sponge cake flavoured with Grand Marnier hides cream, chocolate, and toasted almonds in this domed dessert. *Mocha Whipped Cream Cake (Torta Moka):* a layered cake filled with mocha-flavoured cream and chopped Amaretti biscuits.

ITALIAN COUNTRY MENUS

A traditional Italian meal does not depend on a single course, but is made up of at least two principal dishes, and one or two minor ones as well. A vegetable or salad is always served with the *secondo piatto,* while bread is present at every meal. Here are some ideas for three-course menus drawn from the recipes in this book.

For a simple yet elegant dinner, I'd suggest you begin with fragrant Grilled Mussels with Red Pepper Topping, to be followed by Spinach-Stuffed Veal Rolls. The rolls can be prepared up to 2 days ahead and reheated on the stove, and they make a colourful and attractive presentation when sliced crosswise and arranged on individual plates. For dessert, impress your guests with Ricotta Cheesecake – fresh cheese and almonds, flavoured with orange zest, candied orange peel, and sultanas. What is more, the cheesecake can be completely prepared a day ahead.

Celebrate the approach of summer with a luxurious green Asparagus Risotto. Milanese Veal Escalopes served with sautéed peppers is an equal indulgence, while fresh seasonal berries are combined in Strawberry and Raspberry Hazelnut Tart for a superb finale.

For an autumn dinner, take advantage of seasonal specialities and begin with Baked Polenta with Wild Mushrooms and Fontina, then celebrate the grape harvest with Beef Braised in Red Wine, and bake fresh walnuts in a Walnut Cake with Caramel Topping.

For a simple evening with friends, consider offering Noodles with Sage and Butter followed by Devilled Chicken. Grapefruit or Coffee Granita is a refreshing conclusion, with little All Souls' Day almond biscuits.

ROMAN-STYLE ARTICHOKES WITH HERBS AND GARLIC

Carciofi alla Romana

🍽 SERVES 6 🥄 WORK TIME 25–30 MINUTES 🍲 COOKING TIME 25–45 MINUTES

EQUIPMENT

large heavy-based pan with lid

 slotted spoon

lemon squeezer

 melon baller†

chef's knife

small bowl

small knife

chopping board

†teaspoon can also be used

Young globe artichokes with tender stalks are best for this delicious appetizer that can be served warm or at room temperature. The artichokes are hollowed, and filled with chopped parsley, mint, and garlic, then braised to serve with the stalks upwards. If using older artichokes, you will have to trim away the more fibrous green parts.

GETTING AHEAD
The artichokes can be prepared up to 1 day ahead and refrigerated. Let them come to room temperature before serving.

metric	SHOPPING LIST	imperial
6	garlic cloves	6
1	small bunch of flat-leaf parsley	1
8–10	sprigs of fresh mint, more for decoration	8–10
	salt and pepper	
3	lemons	3
6	young globe artichokes	6
125 ml	olive oil	4 fl oz

INGREDIENTS

garlic cloves

globe artichokes

olive oil

fresh mint

lemons

flat-leaf parsley†

† curly parsley can also be used

ANNE SAYS
"Look for artichokes of medium size, with tender green leaves. The cut stalks should be moist, not dry."

ORDER OF WORK

1 PREPARE THE STUFFING AND ARTICHOKES

2 STUFF AND COOK THE ARTICHOKES

1 PREPARE THE STUFFING AND ARTICHOKES

1 Set the flat side of the chef's knife on top of each garlic clove and strike it with your fist. Discard the skins and finely chop the garlic.

2 Strip the leaves from the parsley and mint stalks. Using the chef's knife, finely chop the leaves.

3 Combine the garlic, chopped parsley and mint, and a little salt in the small bowl. Cut 2 lemons in half, and reserve 1 half for adding to the cooking liquid.

Cut surfaces of lemon will be used to rub over artichokes and help prevent discoloration

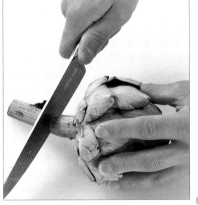

4 Using the chef's knife, trim the tough end of an artichoke stalk, leaving about 4 cm (1½ inches) of stalk.

Prickly ends of artichoke leaves can be sharp

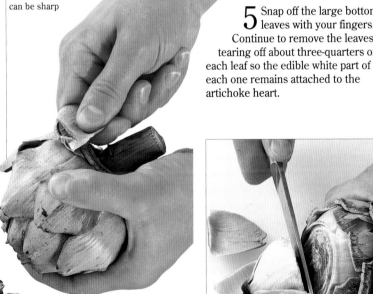

5 Snap off the large bottom leaves with your fingers. Continue to remove the leaves, tearing off about three-quarters of each leaf so the edible white part of each one remains attached to the artichoke heart.

Tough fibres are pulled out of artichoke with leaves

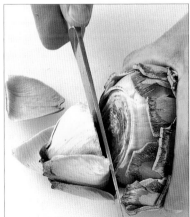

6 Continue until you reach the cone of soft, small leaves in the centre of the artichoke. Trim the cone of leaves with the chef's knife.

7 Rub the cut edges of the artichoke with a lemon half to prevent discoloration, before continuing with the preparation.

ANNE SAYS
"Coat with lemon at once because the artichoke browns rapidly."

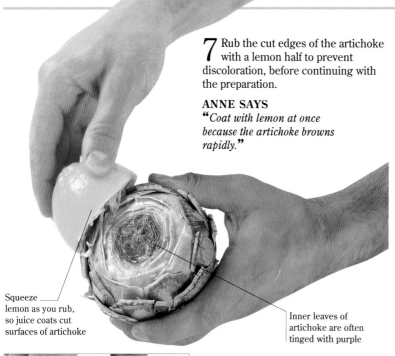

Squeeze lemon as you rub, so juice coats cut surfaces of artichoke

Inner leaves of artichoke are often tinged with purple

8 With the small knife, peel the stalk of the artichoke, cutting away the tough, fibrous exterior.

9 Trim the green parts of the base of the artichoke to remove any of the tough, fibrous leaves.

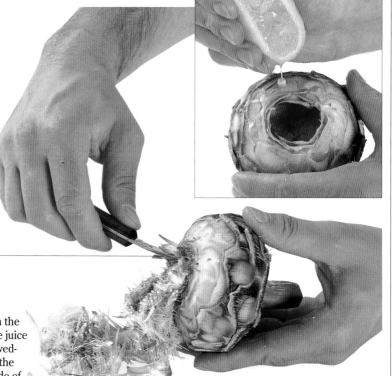

Melon baller makes light work of removing hairy choke

10 Scoop out the choke with the melon baller and squeeze juice from a lemon half into the hollowed-out centre of the artichoke. Rub the juice thoroughly around the inside of the artichoke with your finger. Prepare the remaining artichokes in the same way.

Be sure to remove all central hairy choke thoroughly

2 STUFF AND COOK THE ARTICHOKES

1 Put 2–3 spoonfuls garlic-herb stuffing in the centre of an artichoke and press it down well against the bottom and sides. Stuff the remaining artichokes; you should have 30–45 ml (2–3 tbsp) stuffing left over.

2 Set the artichokes, tops down and stalks up, in the large pan. Sprinkle the remaining stuffing over the outside of the artichokes, and pour the oil over the top.

ANNE SAYS
"The artichokes should just fill the pan in a single layer."

Good quality olive oil adds extra flavour when braising artichokes

3 Sprinkle the artichokes with salt and pepper, and add enough water to come halfway up the sides, not including the stalks.

4 Bring to a boil, then cover the pan and simmer the artichokes 25–45 minutes, depending on their age. Add more water to the pan, if necessary, so the artichokes are always half covered.

Test for tenderness with tip of knife only

5 To test if the artichokes are cooked, pierce them with the point of the small knife; they should be tender.

6 Using the slotted spoon, transfer the artichokes to a large serving dish, arranging them in a single layer, stalks upwards. Boil the cooking liquid in the pan until it is reduced to about 250 ml (8 fl oz).

Cooking liquid is fragrant with herbs, garlic, and olive oil

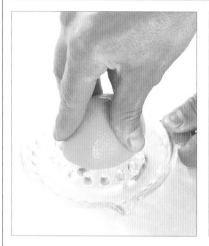

7 With the lemon squeezer, squeeze the juice from the reserved lemon half. Remove any seeds from the lemon juice and discard.

8 Add the lemon juice to the cooking liquid and taste for seasoning. Pour over the artichokes and let cool to room temperature.

9 Meanwhile, cut the remaining lemon into slices with the chef's knife, and set them aside until the artichokes are ready to serve.

⦾ TO SERVE
Serve the artichokes at room temperature, decorated with the lemon slices and sprigs of mint.

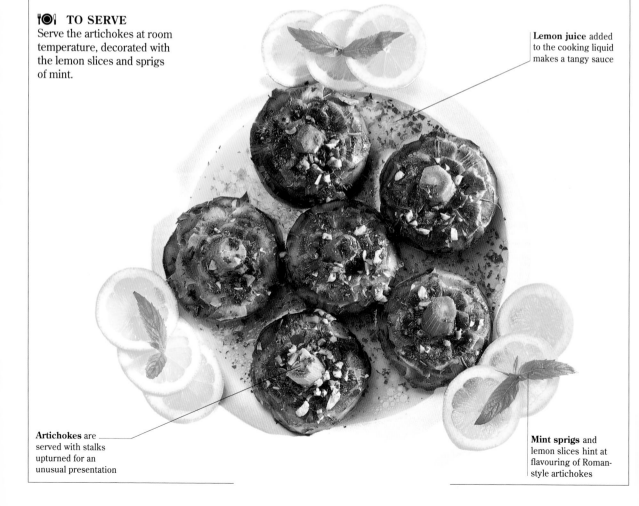

Lemon juice added to the cooking liquid makes a tangy sauce

Artichokes are served with stalks upturned for an unusual presentation

Mint sprigs and lemon slices hint at flavouring of Roman-style artichokes

V A R I A T I O N

SLOW-BRAISED ARTICHOKE HEARTS

In this recipe, called Carciofi in Umido, *artichoke hearts are cut into wedges, then braised with the same seasonings as Roman-Style Artichokes, for a totally different result.*

Artichoke wedges are flavoured with onion, garlic, and herbs

Parsley and mint leaves look dainty together

1 Prepare the herbs and garlic as directed in the main recipe, using only 10–12 sprigs of parsley and 3–5 sprigs of mint; do not mix the garlic and chopped herbs together.
2 Peel 1 small onion, leaving a little of the root attached, and cut it lengthwise in half. Lay each onion half flat on a chopping board and slice horizontally towards the root, leaving the slices attached at the root end, and then slice vertically, again leaving the root end uncut. Finally, cut across the onion to make dice.
3 Prepare the artichoke hearts: remove the stalks by snapping them off so that the fibres are pulled out along with the stalks.
4 Tear off the leaves as directed, then cut off all the soft cone of leaves and remove the choke.
5 Cut each artichoke heart into 8 wedges.

6 Squeeze the juice from 1 lemon into a bowl of water; add the squeezed lemon. Put the artichoke wedges in the acidulated water.
7 Heat 60 ml (4 tbsp) olive oil in a heavy pan, add the onion and garlic, and cook, stirring, until soft, 3–5 minutes.
8 Stir in drained artichoke wedges, parsley, mint, salt, and pepper. Add water to half cover the artichoke wedges and bring to a boil.
9 Press a circle of greaseproof paper on top of the artichokes. Cover the pan and simmer, stirring occasionally, until the artichokes are tender when pierced with a knife, 25–40 minutes, depending on their age. Add more water if necessary, so the artichokes are always half covered.
10 Remove the lid and paper, and bring the cooking liquid to a boil; if necessary, boil until reduced to about 120 ml (4 fl oz). Taste for seasoning and set aside to cool.
11 Serve the artichokes warm or at room temperature in individual bowls. Spoon the cooking liquid over the artichokes and decorate with sprigs of parsley and mint.

GRILLED MUSSELS WITH RED PEPPER TOPPING

Cozze Gratinate

🍴 SERVES 4 🥣 WORK TIME 25–30 MINUTES 🍲 GRILLING TIME 1–2 MINUTES

EQUIPMENT

plastic bag

small brush

food processor †

bowls

large saucepan with lid

small knife

rubber spatula

large baking dish

tongs

slotted spoon

chef's knife

paper towels

chopping board

†blender can also be used

True antipasto! This light dish, to be served before the main course, is perfect for special occasions. The sea-salt flavour of mussels is highlighted by a piquant topping of flat-leaf parsley, garlic, breadcrumbs, and roasted red pepper. This is so delicious that you'll want to make it everyday fare.

GETTING AHEAD

The mussels can be cooked and stuffed up to 4 hours ahead. Keep them, tightly covered, in the refrigerator. Grill them just before serving.

metric	SHOPPING LIST	imperial
1	small bunch of flat-leaf parsley	1
1	large red pepper	1
2	garlic cloves	2
2	slices of white bread	2
30 ml	olive oil	2 tbsp
	salt and pepper	
24	large mussels, total weight about 750 g (1½ lb)	24
250 ml	dry white wine	8 fl oz
1	lemon for serving	1

INGREDIENTS

mussels

flat-leaf parsley †

dry white wine

white bread

olive oil

red pepper

lemon

garlic cloves

†curly parsley can also be used

ANNE SAYS
"You may want to buy a few extra mussels to allow for some damaged shells."

ORDER OF WORK

1 MAKE THE TOPPING

2 PREPARE AND COOK THE MUSSELS

3 STUFF AND GRILL THE MUSSELS

1 MAKE THE TOPPING

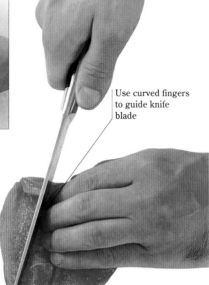

Use curved fingers to guide knife blade

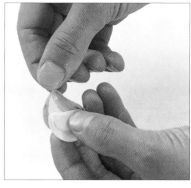

1 Reserving a few sprigs for decoration, strip the parsley leaves from the stalks, keeping both the leaves and stalks separate.

3 To peel the garlic, set the flat side of the chef's knife on each clove and strike it. Discard the skins.

Pepper is sliced so it is easy to work in processor

2 Roast the red pepper (see box, page 18). Cut each pepper half lengthwise into strips.

ANNE SAYS
"*The pepper strips will be worked in the food processor, so it is not necessary to cut them neatly.*"

4 Using the chef's knife, trim and discard the crusts from the bread slices. Cut the bread into cubes.

ITALIAN HERBS

A visit to any Italian vegetable market demonstrates the country's abundance of fresh herbs. Oregano, basil, and flat-leaf parsley, in particular, are used widely in Italian cooking.

Oregano, *which is actually a wild variety of marjoram, is native to the Mediterranean region. It has a more pronounced flavour than marjoram, and appears in many Italian dishes, especially tomato sauces, stews, and pizza. It can be used fresh or dried.*

Basil *is one of the most important herbs in Italian cooking. It goes with many foods, but has a special affinity with tomatoes – a favourite Italian salad is torn fresh basil leaves scattered over sliced tomatoes drizzled with fruity extra-virgin olive oil. It is best to use fresh basil when specified in recipes because dried basil does not have the same flavour – it tastes more minty. Italian cooks preserve their summer basil crops by filling jars with the leaves, lightly salting them, then topping up with olive oil.*

Flat-Leaf Parsley *is native to southern Europe, and widely used in Italian cooking. Flat-leaf parsley is preferred by Italian cooks to curly parsley because it has a deeper, more pungent flavour, and because it stands up far better to heat in cooked dishes. However, both types are interchangeable in recipes, so if you find curly parsley easier to obtain, it can be substituted wherever flat-leaf parsley is specified.*

5 Work the cubes of bread in the food processor to form crumbs. Add the parsley leaves, peeled garlic cloves, olive oil, and the roasted red pepper strips to the food processor.

Food processor makes it quick and easy to chop ingredients for topping

Flat-leaf parsley has robust flavour

6 Work the ingredients to a purée. Season the mixture to taste with salt and pepper. Alternatively, chop the parsley leaves, garlic, and roasted red pepper by hand with the chef's knife, then stir in the breadcrumbs and oil; you will have a coarser topping.

HOW TO ROAST, PEEL, AND SEED PEPPERS

Roasting peppers under the grill makes them easy to peel and gives them a smoky flavour. After they are roasted, peeled, and cored, peppers can be stuffed whole, sliced and added to salads, or cooked alone or with other vegetables.

1 Heat the grill. Set the whole pepper on a rack about 10 cm (4 inches) from the heat. Grill the pepper, turning as needed, until the skin is black and blistered all over, 10–12 minutes.

2 Seal the pepper in a plastic bag and let cool so the skin is loosened by the steam trapped inside.

Roasted peppers are tender and full of flavour

Flatten pepper half so seeds are easy to scrape off

3 With a small knife, peel off the skin. Rinse the pepper under running water and pat dry with paper towels.

4 Cut out the core, then slit pepper lengthwise in half. Scrape out seeds and white ribs with the knife blade.

2 PREPARE AND COOK THE MUSSELS

1 Clean the mussels: scrape them with the small knife to remove any barnacles.

Back of knife is used for scraping off barnacles

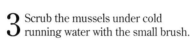

Shells are cleaned to make attractive presentation

2 Using the small knife, detach and discard any weeds or "beards" from the mussels.

3 Scrub the mussels under cold running water with the small brush.

4 Discard any mussels that have broken shells or that do not close when tapped.

! TAKE CARE !
Only cook mussels that are in good condition.

Stir mussels once during cooking so they steam evenly

5 Put the wine and parsley stalks in the saucepan. Bring to a boil and simmer 2 minutes. Add the mussels.

6 Cover and cook over high heat, stirring once, until the mussels open, 2–3 minutes. Transfer them to a large bowl with the slotted spoon. Discard any mussels that have not opened at this point.

Parsley stalks add flavour to cooking liquid

ANNE SAYS
"If you like, strain the flavourful cooking liquid from mussels to use as fish stock."

3 STUFF AND GRILL THE MUSSELS

1 Heat the grill. Remove the top shell from each mussel and discard the rubbery ring surrounding the meat.

2 Using a teaspoon, spoon a little of the roasted pepper topping onto each of the mussels.

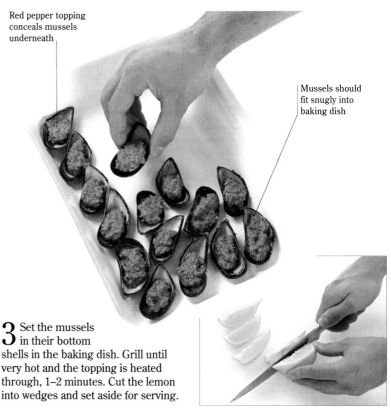

Red pepper topping conceals mussels underneath

Mussels should fit snugly into baking dish

3 Set the mussels in their bottom shells in the baking dish. Grill until very hot and the topping is heated through, 1–2 minutes. Cut the lemon into wedges and set aside for serving.

🍴 **TO SERVE**
Arrange the mussels, fanned in circles, on warmed individual plates, with a lemon wedge on the side of each. Decorate with a parsley sprig.

Lemon juice is delicious on piping hot mussels

Red pepper topping makes colourful contrast to black mussel shells

VARIATION
GRILLED CLAMS

Amande clams are featured here in Vongole Gratinate, *although Venus clams are a delicious alternative.*

1 Make the roasted pepper topping as directed in the main recipe.
2 Substitute 36 small or 24 medium undamaged live clams for the mussels and scrub them; unlike mussels, clams do not have barnacles or weeds.

3 Cook the clams as directed in the main recipe, allowing 3–5 minutes for the clams to open, or longer if the shells are very thick.
4 Meanwhile, thinly slice a lemon for decoration. Cut each lemon slice from centre to edge, and twist each edge in opposite directions.
5 Discard the black skin covering the neck of each clam, nipping it off with your fingers. Spoon the topping over the clams and grill them as directed.
6 Serve them on warmed individual plates. Decorate each plate with a lemon twist and parsley sprigs.

VARIATION
GRILLED MUSSELS WITH PARSLEY AND CAPERS

Capers replace the roasted red pepper in Cozze al Prezzemolo e Capperi.

Lemon slices are refreshing decoration

Caper topping is piquant complement to mussels

1 Omit the red pepper from the main recipe. Peel 4 garlic cloves; drain 15 ml (1 tbsp) capers in a small strainer.
2 Make the topping as directed, adding 30 ml (2 tbsp) grated Parmesan cheese to the breadcrumbs, with the garlic, parsley, and oil; replace the pepper with the capers. Taste for seasoning.

Capers add piquancy

3 Steam the mussels and remove the top shells as directed. Spoon the topping over the mussels.

4 Arrange the mussels in gratin dishes and sprinkle with 30 ml (2 tbsp) grated Parmesan cheese; grill as directed. Decorate with half slices of lemon.

BAKED POLENTA WITH WILD MUSHROOMS AND FONTINA

Polenta Pasticciata

 SERVES 6   WORK TIME 40–45 MINUTES*   BAKING TIME 20–25 MINUTES

EQUIPMENT

large saucepan

medium frying pan

paper towels

palette knife

baking sheets

bowls

wooden spoon

small knife

whisk

chef's knife

pastry brush

baking dish

chopping board

Polenta was once daily fare in parts of Italy, so there are many tempting recipes for it. Here it is sliced and baked with wild mushrooms and cheese.

GETTING AHEAD
The dish can be prepared up to 1 day ahead and refrigerated. Bake as directed in the recipe.

*plus 1 hour chilling time

metric	SHOPPING LIST	imperial
1.5 litres	water	2⅓ pints
15 ml	salt	1 tbsp
375 g	fine cornmeal	12 oz
	For the wild mushroom stew	
250 g	fresh wild mushrooms, such as chanterelles or boletus, or 60 g (2 oz) dried wild mushrooms	8 oz
375 g	common mushrooms	12 oz
3	garlic cloves	3
5–7	sprigs of fresh thyme or rosemary	5–7
45 ml	olive oil, more for baking dish	3 tbsp
125 ml	dry white wine	4 fl oz
250 ml	beef stock (see box, page 122) or water	8 fl oz
60 ml	double cream	4 tbsp
	salt and pepper	
250 g	fontina cheese	8 oz

INGREDIENTS

fresh chanterelles   common mushrooms

fresh thyme   fontina cheese†

fine cornmeal   olive oil   dry white wine

double cream

 beef stock

garlic cloves

†mozzarella, Gouda, or Edam can also be used

ANNE SAYS
"If using dried mushrooms, soak in 250 ml (8 fl oz) warm water until plump. Drain, and reserve liquid."

ORDER OF WORK

1 MAKE THE POLENTA

2 MAKE THE MUSHROOM STEW

3 BAKE THE PASTICCIATA

1 MAKE THE POLENTA

1 Sprinkle 2 baking sheets with water. Bring the 1.5 litres (2¹/₃ pints) water to a boil in the saucepan and add the salt. Over medium heat, slowly whisk in the cornmeal in a thin, steady stream.

! TAKE CARE !
Be sure the heat is not too high, and whisk constantly to avoid lumps.

Add cornmeal slowly, to prevent lumps forming

2 Cook the mixture, stirring to prevent sticking, until thick enough to pull away from the side of the pan, 10–15 minutes. The polenta mixture should be soft and smooth.

3 Spread the polenta evenly on the baking sheets, in a layer about 30 cm (12 inches) square and 1 cm (³/₈ inch) thick on each sheet. Let cool, then chill until very firm, 1 hour.

2 MAKE THE MUSHROOM STEW

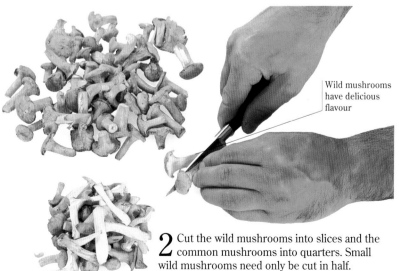

Wild mushrooms have delicious flavour

1 Wipe the fresh wild mushrooms and common mushrooms with damp paper towels, and trim the stalks.

2 Cut the wild mushrooms into slices and the common mushrooms into quarters. Small wild mushrooms need only be cut in half.

3 Set the flat side of the chef's knife on top of each garlic clove and strike it with your fist. Discard the skins and finely chop the garlic. Strip the thyme leaves from the stalks.

4 Heat the oil in the frying pan. Add all of the mushrooms, garlic, and thyme and cook, stirring, until the mushrooms are tender and the liquid has evaporated, 5–7 minutes.

Double cream binds mushroom stew

Mushroom mixture is rich and juicy

5 Add the wine and simmer until almost evaporated, 2–3 minutes. Add the stock or water if using fresh wild mushrooms (or the soaking liquid if using dried mushrooms) and continue cooking until reduced by half, 5–7 minutes. Stir in the cream until the liquid thickens slightly, 1–2 minutes. Season to taste with salt and pepper.

3 BAKE THE PASTICCIATA

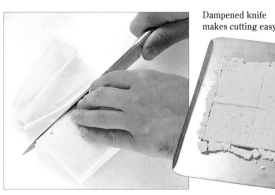

Dampened knife makes cutting easy

1 Heat the oven to 220°C (425°F, Gas 7). Brush a 23 x 33 cm (9 x 13 inch) baking dish with olive oil. Cut the fontina cheese into thin, even slices, discarding the rind.

2 Cut the chilled polenta on each baking sheet into 6 even-sized pieces. Trim them into 10 cm (4 inch) squares so they will fit evenly in the baking dish; reserve the trimmings.

3 Arrange half of the polenta squares in the bottom of the prepared baking dish, placing them side by side in a single layer.

4 Spoon half of the mushroom stew over the polenta, spreading the mushrooms evenly over the squares.

Polenta squares will absorb liquid from mushrooms

Fontina cheese melts into mushroom mixture

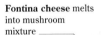

5 Arrange half of the sliced fontina on top. Repeat with another layer of the remaining polenta and mushrooms. Cut the polenta trimmings into small squares and arrange them over the mushrooms. Top with the remaining fontina slices. Bake the pasticciata in the heated oven until the cheese is melted and the polenta and mushrooms are very hot, 20–25 minutes.

🍽 **TO SERVE**
Transfer squares of pasticciata directly from the baking dish onto 6 warmed plates.

Wild mushroom stew and mild fontina cheese make a delicious combination of flavours

BAKED POLENTA WITH PARMA HAM AND EGGS

In Polenta Pasticciata con Prosciutto e Uova, *polenta is baked with diced Parma ham, beaten eggs, and grated Parmesan.*

1 Make the polenta as directed in the main recipe, using 300 g (10 oz) cornmeal and 1.25 litres (2 pints) water. Spread the polenta on 2 moistened baking sheets, as directed, and let cool; chill until firm. Cut the polenta into twelve 10 cm (4 inch) squares.
2 Omit the wild mushroom stew and fontina cheese. Chop 125 g (4 oz) thinly sliced Parma ham. Beat 2 eggs and season them with pepper.
3 Brush a 20 cm (8 inch) square dish with olive oil. Arrange one-third of the polenta squares in the dish and spoon over half of the beaten egg. Sprinkle with half of the chopped Parma ham and 30 g (1 oz) freshly grated Parmesan cheese.
4 Top with half of the remaining polenta, the remaining egg and Parma ham, and 30 g (1 oz) Parmesan cheese. Arrange the remaining polenta squares on top and sprinkle with another 30 g (1 oz) Parmesan cheese.
5 Bake as directed, until the top is golden brown. Serves 4.

STRAW AND HAY PASTA WITH CREAM, HAM, AND MUSHROOMS

Paglia e Fieno alla Ghiottona

🍽 SERVES 6 🥄 WORK TIME 55–60 MINUTES* 🍲 COOKING TIME 2–4 MINUTES

EQUIPMENT

pasta machine

wooden spoon

chef's knife

large frying pan

large forks

colander

palette knife

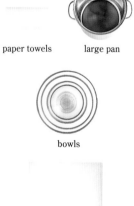

paper towels   large pan

bowls

chopping board

This dish of green and white fettuccine (representing straw and hay), ham, mushrooms, and peas in a cream sauce would appeal to any gourmand, or ghiottone *in Italian.*

plus 3–4 hours standing time

INGREDIENTS

cooked ham

Parmesan cheese

strong flour

eggs

ground nutmeg

frozen spinach

onion

fresh peas

double cream

mushrooms   butter

metric	SHOPPING LIST	imperial
250 g	mushrooms	8 oz
125 g	sliced cooked ham	4 oz
1	small onion	1
60 g	butter	2 oz
100 g	shelled fresh peas or defrosted peas	3 ½ oz
250 ml	double cream	8 fl oz
1	pinch of ground nutmeg	1
60 g	freshly grated Parmesan cheese for serving	2 oz
	salt and pepper	
	For the plain fettuccine	
150 g	strong plain flour, more if needed	5 oz
2	eggs	2
	For the spinach fettuccine	
30 ml	defrosted spinach	2 tbsp
220 g	strong plain flour, more if needed	7 oz
2	eggs	2

ORDER OF WORK

1 MAKE THE PLAIN AND SPINACH PASTA DOUGH

2 KNEAD, ROLL, AND CUT THE PASTA

3 PREPARE SAUCE

4 COOK THE PASTA

1 MAKE THE PLAIN AND SPINACH PASTA DOUGH

Use fingertips to mix dough

1 Make the plain pasta dough: sift the flour onto a work surface in a mound, using a sieve or a flour sifter. With your fingers, make a well in the centre of the flour.

2 Lightly beat the eggs with a fork and add to the well in the flour, with 2.5 ml (½ tsp) salt.

3 Gradually mix in the flour from the sides to make a firm dough. If the dough is sticky, add more flour.

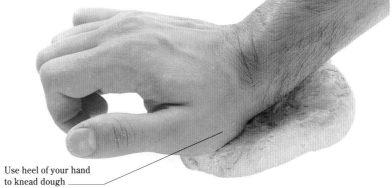

Use heel of your hand to knead dough

4 As you mix, use the palette knife to scrape up bits of dough that stick to the work surface.

ANNE SAYS
"The dough may appear dry and floury at first, but will become more moist as the flour absorbs the eggs."

5 On a floured work surface, press the dough together into a ball. Knead it with the heel of your hand to blend. Cover the dough with a bowl and leave to rest, 1 hour. Meanwhile, make the spinach pasta dough.

ANNE SAYS
"If you are short of time or do not have a pasta machine, you can substitute 500 g (1 lb) fresh or dried bought fettuccine, cooking it 1–2 minutes for fresh, 7–10 minutes for dried, or according to package directions."

6 For the spinach pasta dough: squeeze the defrosted spinach in your fist to remove all excess water. Finely chop it with the chef's knife.

7 Make the pasta dough as for the plain dough, adding the spinach with the eggs and salt. Leave the dough to rest, covered with a bowl, 1 hour.

Spinach dough is green, representing hay

Plain pasta dough is light gold like straw

2 KNEAD, ROLL, AND CUT THE PASTA

1 Using the palette knife, cut the ball of spinach dough into 3 or 4 pieces of more or less equal size. Set the pasta machine rollers on their widest setting.

2 Flour 1 piece of spinach dough lightly and feed it through the rollers of the machine.

3 Fold the dough strip into thirds or quarters to make a square, then feed it through the machine rollers again, dusting with flour if the dough sticks. Repeat this folding and rolling process 7–10 times to knead the dough until it is smooth and elastic.

4 Tighten the pasta machine rollers 1 notch and feed the dough through them.

5 Continue rolling the pasta dough, tightening the rollers 1 notch each time, ending with the rollers on their narrowest setting.

Catch dough as it comes through rollers

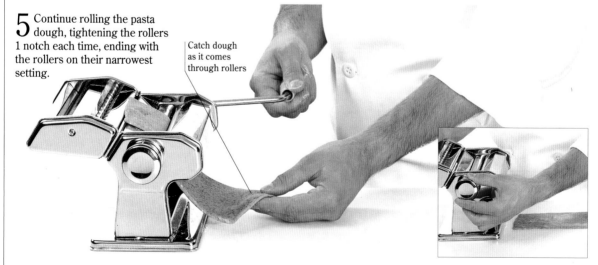

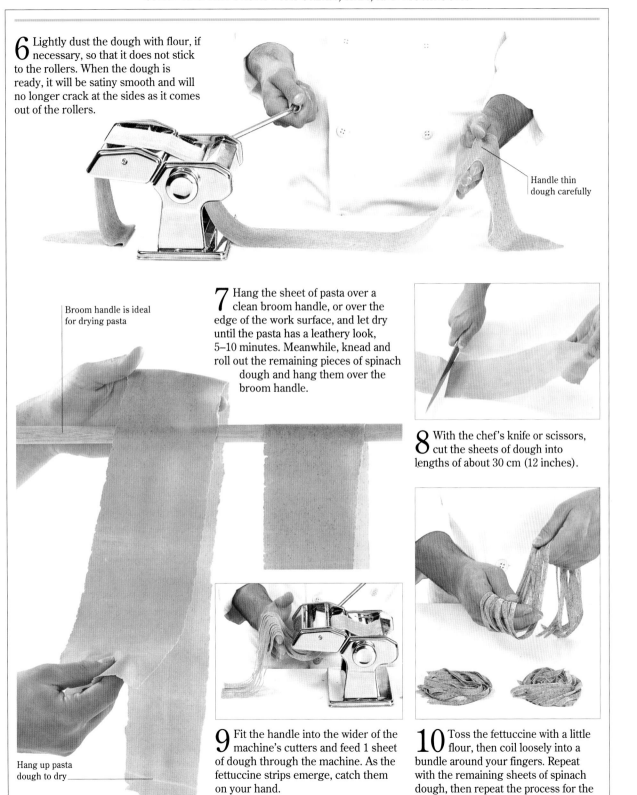

6 Lightly dust the dough with flour, if necessary, so that it does not stick to the rollers. When the dough is ready, it will be satiny smooth and will no longer crack at the sides as it comes out of the rollers.

Handle thin dough carefully

Broom handle is ideal for drying pasta

7 Hang the sheet of pasta over a clean broom handle, or over the edge of the work surface, and let dry until the pasta has a leathery look, 5–10 minutes. Meanwhile, knead and roll out the remaining pieces of spinach dough and hang them over the broom handle.

8 With the chef's knife or scissors, cut the sheets of dough into lengths of about 30 cm (12 inches).

Hang up pasta dough to dry

9 Fit the handle into the wider of the machine's cutters and feed 1 sheet of dough through the machine. As the fettuccine strips emerge, catch them on your hand.

10 Toss the fettuccine with a little flour, then coil loosely into a bundle around your fingers. Repeat with the remaining sheets of spinach dough, then repeat the process for the plain pasta dough. Let dry, 1–2 hours.

3 PREPARE SAUCE

1 Wipe the mushroom caps with damp paper towels and trim the stalks even with the caps. Set the mushrooms stalk-side down and slice them.

2 Cut the ham into thin strips. Peel the onion and cut it lengthwise in half. Slice each half horizontally, then vertically. Cut into fine dice.

Double cream thickens sauce

3 Heat half of the butter in the large frying pan. Add the onion and cook, stirring occasionally with the wooden spoon, until soft, 3–5 minutes. Add the sliced mushrooms with salt and pepper and continue cooking until the liquid evaporates, 5–7 minutes.

4 Add the ham strips, peas, and double cream to the onions and mushrooms. Stir and heat to boiling, then simmer until slightly reduced, 1–2 minutes. Add the ground nutmeg to the sauce and taste for seasoning.

4 COOK THE PASTA

1 Fill the large pan with water, bring to a boil, and add 15 ml (1 tbsp) salt. Add the plain and spinach fettuccine and simmer until just tender but still chewy, 1–2 minutes, stirring occasionally to prevent sticking.

ANNE SAYS
"Test by tasting the pasta – it should be chewy, or al dente."

Water loses heat momentarily when pasta is added

2 Drain the fettuccine thoroughly in the colander, rinse with hot water to wash away the starch, and drain again thoroughly.

Toss pasta in
butter before
adding sauce

3 Melt the remaining
butter in the pan and
add the fettuccine. Toss with
the butter over medium heat,
then add the sauce, and continue
tossing until coated and very hot,
1–2 minutes. Take from the heat,
sprinkle generously with some of the
freshly grated Parmesan cheese, and
toss again.

Parmesan cheese
is sprinkled on top
of each serving as
a finishing touch

🍽 **TO SERVE**
Pile the pasta in warmed individual
bowls and serve with the
remaining Parmesan
cheese.

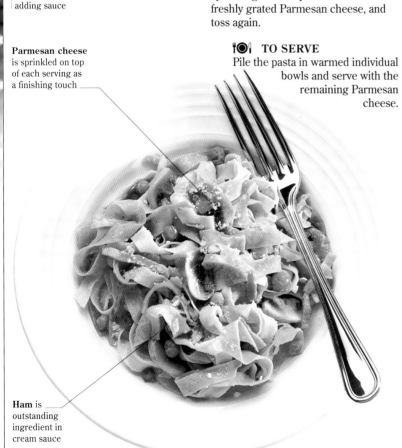

Ham is
outstanding
ingredient in
cream sauce

VARIATION

NOODLES WITH SAGE AND BUTTER

*In this version of straw and hay
pasta,* Tonnarelli al Salvia e
Burro, *skinny noodles replace
the fettuccine, tossed with
chopped fresh sage and melted
butter.*

1 Make, knead, and roll the plain and
spinach pasta dough as directed,
ending with the rollers at the third
narrowest setting; the dough should be
about 3 mm (1/8 inch) thick.
2 Cut the dough into 15 cm (6 inch)
lengths, then cut them with the pasta
machine, using the narrower of the
machine's cutters – they should be the
shape of squared-off spaghetti. Dry the
noodles as directed in the main recipe.
3 Omit the cream sauce. Strip the
leaves from 1 medium bunch of fresh
sage and pile them on a chopping
board. With a chef's knife, coarsely
chop the leaves.
4 Cook and drain the pasta and put it
in a warmed serving bowl. Add 125 g
(4 oz) butter, cut into small pieces, and
sprinkle the chopped sage on the top.
5 Toss until all the strands of pasta are
coated with melted butter and chopped
sage. Season with salt and pepper.
Serve freshly grated Parmesan cheese
separately.

GETTING AHEAD

The fettuccine can be made, dried, and stored, loosely wrapped,
in the refrigerator up to 48 hours, or they can be frozen. Sprinkle
them lightly with flour so that the pieces do not stick together.
Prepare the sauce and cook the fettuccine just before serving.

PRAWN RISOTTO

Risotto ai Gamberi

🍴 SERVES 6 🥣 WORK TIME 15–20 MINUTES ☕ COOKING TIME 25–30 MINUTES*

EQUIPMENT

chef's knife

small knife small bowl

saucepans

wooden spoon

ladle

slotted spoon

chopping board

The best risotto is made with short-grain Italian Arborio rice, simmered until al dente – smooth and creamy but slightly firm to the bite. Stock is added gradually and you must stir constantly – tedious, but the results are well worth it. Once the risotto is made, do not leave it to stand or it will become heavy.

GETTING AHEAD

Freshly made risotto is incomparable; there is really no satisfactory way to reheat it or keep it warm.

*At no time during the cooking of the risotto can you leave the kitchen, as the risotto must be stirred constantly. This is most important to remember when calculating your total work time.

INGREDIENTS

raw prawns Arborio rice†

fish stock flat-leaf parsley ‡

garlic cloves

dry white wine olive oil

onion

†other short-grain or medium-grain rice can also be used

‡curly parsley can also be used

ANNE SAYS
"Do not worry if you are short of stock. You can use more water instead, adding just a small amount of stock to flavour the risotto."

ORDER OF WORK

1 PREPARE THE PRAWNS AND COOKING LIQUID

2 COOK THE RICE AND ADD THE PRAWNS

ANNE SAYS
"Make sure that the saucepan you use for cooking the rice is large enough to allow room for expansion. A heavy-based saucepan is essential, to prevent the rice sticking to the bottom."

metric	SHOPPING LIST	imperial
500 g	small or medium raw prawns	1 lb
2	garlic cloves	2
1	small bunch of flat-leaf parsley	1
90 ml	olive oil	3 fl oz
	salt and pepper	
60 ml	dry white wine	4 tbsp
1 litre	fish or chicken stock (see boxes, page 123)	1²/₃ pints
250 ml	water, more if needed	8 fl oz
1	medium onion	1
420 g	Arborio rice	14 oz

1 PREPARE THE PRAWNS AND COOKING LIQUID

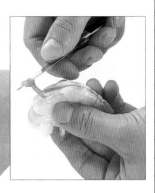

Prawn shells come off easily in your fingers

1 Peel off the prawn shells with your fingers. Make a shallow cut along the back of each peeled prawn with the small knife and remove the dark intestinal vein.

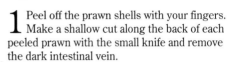

2 Set the flat side of the chef's knife on top of each garlic clove and strike it with your fist. Peel and finely chop the garlic. Strip the parsley leaves from the stalks, reserving 6 sprigs for garnish. Pile the leaves on the chopping board and coarsely chop them with the chef's knife.

3 Heat one-third of the oil in a medium saucepan and add the garlic, parsley, peeled prawns, salt, and pepper.

Pink prawns are perfumed with garlic, parsley, and white wine

4 Cook, stirring with the slotted spoon, just until the prawns turn pink, 1–2 minutes. Pour in the wine and stir thoroughly.

5 Transfer the prawns to the bowl; set aside. Simmer the liquid in the pan until reduced by three-quarters, 2–3 minutes. Add the stock and 250 ml (8 fl oz) water to the liquid and heat to boiling. Keep the liquid simmering.

2 COOK THE RICE AND ADD THE PRAWNS

1 Peel the onion, leaving a little of the root attached, and cut lengthwise in half. Slice each half horizontally towards the root, leaving the slices attached at the root end. Then slice vertically, again leaving the root end uncut. Cut across the onion to make dice.

2 Heat half of the remaining oil in a large saucepan. Add the onion and cook, stirring with the wooden spoon, until soft but not brown, 2–3 minutes.

3 Add the rice to the pan and stir until shiny and coated with oil. Using the ladle, pour in just enough of the simmering liquid to cover the rice.

4 Simmer the rice, stirring constantly until all the liquid is absorbed, 3–5 minutes. Add more liquid just to cover the rice and simmer, stirring, until completely absorbed.

Rice will start absorbing liquid quickly

Liquid for risotto can be fish stock or chicken stock

5 Continue adding liquid to the rice in this way. Stir constantly, and make sure all the liquid is absorbed before adding more.

Prawns give
flavour to
creamy rice

6 Test the rice from time to time towards the end of the cooking. Stop adding liquid when the rice is *al dente* – just tender but firm to the bite. The total cooking time should be 25–30 minutes, and you will need 1–1.25 litres (1²/₃–2 pints) liquid altogether, adding more water if necessary. Stir in the prawns and the remaining olive oil, and season with salt and pepper to taste.

ANNE SAYS
"As soon as the rice is tender, stop adding liquid, because you do not want the final result to be too soupy."

TO SERVE
Spoon the risotto into warmed bowls, garnish with the reserved parsley sprigs and serve immediately.

Perfectly cooked risotto is creamily bound together, neither stiff nor soupy

Fresh prawns
add luxurious touch
to traditional risotto

VARIATION

ASPARAGUS RISOTTO

Tender green asparagus sautéed in butter is the basis for Risotto con gli Asparagi.

1 Omit the garlic, parsley, prawns, white wine, and onion. Peel 2 shallots, if necessary separating the shallots into sections and peeling the sections. On a chopping board, finely dice them.
2 Peel the tough outer skin from 500 g (1 lb) asparagus and trim off woody ends. Cut the asparagus into 1.25 cm (½ inch) lengths; set aside the tips.
3 Heat 1.25 litres (2 pints) mild chicken stock in a pan to simmering. Heat about 45 ml (3 tbsp) olive oil in a second pan, cook the shallots, stirring until soft but not brown, 1–2 minutes.
4 Add the asparagus stalks to the shallots, cover the pan, and sauté until they are tender, 2–3 minutes.
5 Stir in the rice as directed. Cook, adding the simmering stock as directed.
6 Add the reserved asparagus tips with the second-to-last batch of liquid; cook about 10 minutes. If you like, some asparagus tips can be cooked separately for a garnish. Add them to boiling salted water, cook until tender, 2–3 minutes, drain, and set aside.
7 When the rice is tender, stir in 30 g (1 oz) butter and taste for seasoning. Serve at once in warmed individual bowls, topped with freshly grated Parmesan cheese. Garnish with asparagus tips, if you like.

QUILLS WITH SPICY TOMATO AND BACON SAUCE

Penne all'Arrabbiata

🍲 SERVES 6   🥣 WORK TIME 35–40 MINUTES   🍲 COOKING TIME 30–40 MINUTES

EQUIPMENT

chef's knife

small knife

large pan

bowls

paper towels

large frying pan with lid

wooden spoon

colander

slotted spoon

saucepan

chopping board

rubber gloves

On the whole, Italians do not savour spicy foods, but this is an exception. Here, it is red chilli that brings a dose of fire to the spicy tomato sauce. With bacon and mushrooms, it coats the pasta, traditionally served as a first course.

GETTING AHEAD

The tomato and bacon sauce can be made up to 2 days ahead and refrigerated. Reheat it on top of the stove and cook the pasta just before serving.

INGREDIENTS

quills   plum tomatoes

Parmesan cheese†

fresh oregano   thick-cut bacon rashers

butter

mushrooms

fresh red chilli‡

garlic cloves

† Pecorino cheese can also be used
‡ dried red chilli can also be used

ANNE SAYS
"Out of season, I often substitute canned whole plum tomatoes for fresh ones, reserving their juice."

ORDER OF WORK

1   **MAKE THE SPICY TOMATO AND BACON SAUCE**

2   **COOK THE QUILLS; FINISH THE DISH**

metric	SHOPPING LIST	imperial
500 g	quills	1 lb
30 g	butter	1 oz
60 g	freshly grated Parmesan cheese	2 oz
	For the spicy tomato and bacon sauce	
1.4 kg	plum or medium tomatoes	3 lb
1	fresh red chilli	1
2	garlic cloves	2
375 g	mushrooms	12 oz
5–7	sprigs of fresh oregano	5–7
125 g	thick-cut bacon rashers	4 oz
	salt and pepper	

1 MAKE THE SPICY TOMATO AND BACON SAUCE

1 Remove the cores from the tomatoes and score an "x" on the base of each. Immerse in a pan of boiling water until the skins start to split, 8–15 seconds, depending on their ripeness. Transfer to cold water. When cold, peel off the skins, cut the tomatoes crosswise in half, squeeze out the seeds, then coarsely chop each half.

Plum tomatoes are ideal when available

2 Wearing rubber gloves, cut the fresh chilli lengthwise in half with the small knife. Cut out the core and fleshy white ribs; scrape out the seeds. Cut each half into very thin strips. Hold the strips together, and cut across to make fine dice. If using a dried chilli, chop it and discard the seeds.

3 Set the flat side of the chef's knife on top of each garlic clove and strike it with your fist. Discard the skins and finely chop the garlic.

Whole oregano leaves make attractive garnish

4 Wipe the mushrooms with damp paper towels, trim the stalks even with the caps. Set the mushrooms stalk-side down and slice them.

ANNE SAYS
"I often buy a selection of different mushrooms for added flavour."

5 Strip the oregano leaves from the stalks, reserving a few leaves for garnish. Pile the leaves on the chopping board and finely chop them.

6 Stack the bacon rashers on the chopping board and cut across into wide strips, using the chef's knife.

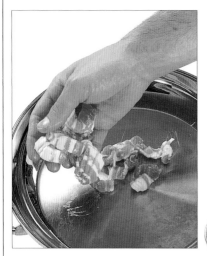

Bacon adds smoky flavour to tomato sauce

7 Transfer the bacon strips to the frying pan. Fry over low heat, stirring occasionally, until the bacon is lightly browned and the fat is rendered (melted), 5–7 minutes.

8 Spoon off most of the fat, leaving about 45 ml (3 tbsp) in which to sauté the mushrooms.

9 Increase the heat, and add the mushrooms to the pan. Cook, stirring with the wooden spoon, until mushrooms have softened and most of the liquid has evaporated, 3–5 minutes.

10 Add the garlic, chilli, oregano, chopped tomatoes with any juice, salt, and pepper. Bring to a boil, cover with a lid, and simmer, stirring occasionally, until the sauce is thick and rich, 25–30 minutes.

Fresh tomatoes will cook down to rich pulp

11 If necessary to thicken the sauce, continue to cook, without the lid, a few minutes longer. Taste the sauce for seasoning.

2 COOK THE QUILLS; FINISH THE DISH

2 Drain the quills in the colander and rinse with hot water to wash away any starch. Drain the quills again thoroughly.

🍽 TO SERVE

Transfer the quills to a warmed serving bowl and add the butter. Toss together with 2 large forks until well coated. Spoon over the sauce, and half of the grated cheese. Toss together, then sprinkle over a little more cheese and garnish with the reserved oregano leaves. Serve immediately, with the remaining cheese.

1 Fill the large pan with cold water, bring to a boil, and add 15 ml (1 tbsp) salt. Add the quills. Simmer until *al dente*, tender but still chewy, 5–8 minutes, stirring occasionally.

Quill-shaped pasta
holds plenty of sauce

Tomato sauce can be made extra spicy by adding more chilli

VARIATION

SPAGHETTI WITH TOMATO AND CHILLI SAUCE

Spaghetti alla Satana is a perfect description for this dish, which is even spicier than Penne all'Arrabbiata.

1 Omit the bacon, mushrooms, and oregano from the main recipe. Peel, seed, and chop 1.4 kg (3 lb) tomatoes, plum or medium, as directed.
2 Chop 2 fresh or dried red chillies, discarding the seeds. Peel and chop 4 garlic cloves.
3 Heat 45 ml (3 tbsp) olive oil in a frying pan, add the chopped chillies and garlic, and sauté just until fragrant, about 30 seconds.
4 Add the chopped tomatoes, salt, and pepper and continue as directed.
5 Cook 500 g (1 lb) dried spaghetti as for the quills. Drain and rinse the spaghetti, then toss with the sauce until thoroughly coated.
6 Serve on warmed individual plates, sprinkled with Parmesan cheese.

BAKED RIGATONI WITH MEATBALLS

Timballo di Rigatoni

🍽 SERVES 6–8   🥣 WORK TIME 45–50 MINUTES   ♨ BAKING TIME 30–40 MINUTES

EQUIPMENT

food processor †

colander

slotted spoon

palette knife

chef's knife

large frying pan

pastry brush

small knife

bowls

large metal spoon

wooden spoon

grater

large saucepans

chopping board

2 litre
(3¼ pint)
soufflé dish

rubber spatula

† blender can also be used

In this family favourite, rigatoni and tomato-basil sauce are embellished with small meatballs, then baked with a topping of Parmesan cheese. Italians like to use finger-length macaroni called mezzani, *but other tubular pasta, such as* penne *or short macaroni, are fine alternatives.*

GETTING AHEAD

The pasta can be baked 1 day ahead and kept refrigerated. Reheat it in a 190°C (375°F, Gas 5) oven, 15–20 minutes.

metric	SHOPPING LIST	imperial
3	garlic cloves	3
1	medium bunch of fresh basil	1
1.4 kg	fresh plum or medium tomatoes	3 lb
	salt and pepper	
375 g	tubular pasta (rigatoni, penne, or macaroni)	12 oz
	For the meatballs	
3–5	sprigs of flat-leaf parsley	3–5
500 g	lean minced beef	1 lb
125 g	freshly grated Parmesan cheese	4 oz
	juice of ½ lemon	
1	egg	1
45 ml	olive oil, more for soufflé dish	3 tbsp

INGREDIENTS

tubular pasta

Parmesan cheese

lemon juice

fresh basil

minced beef

plum tomatoes †

flat-leaf parsley ‡

garlic cloves

olive oil

egg

† 840 g (28 oz) canned plum tomatoes can also be used
‡ curly parsley can also be used

ORDER OF WORK

1   MAKE THE TOMATO-BASIL SAUCE

2   MAKE THE MEATBALLS

3   COOK, ASSEMBLE, AND BAKE THE RIGATONI

MAKE THE TOMATO-BASIL SAUCE

HOW TO CHOP HERBS

Basil, parsley, dill, chives, rosemary, and tarragon are herbs that are usually chopped before being added to other ingredients. Do not chop delicate herbs like basil too finely because they bruise easily.

1 Separate the garlic cloves from the bulb. Peel and finely chop the garlic (see box, page 42). Chop the basil leaves (see box, right).

2 Cut the cores from fresh tomatoes and score an "x" on the base of each with the tip of the small knife. Immerse them, a few at a time, in a saucepan of boiling water until the skins start to split, 8–15 seconds, depending on their ripeness.

Tomatoes immersed in cold water quickly become cool enough to handle

1 Strip the leaves or sprigs from the stalks. Pile the leaves or sprigs on a chopping board.

Chop basil leaves coarsely to avoid bruising them

Tomato skins peel off easily after scalding

3 Using the slotted spoon, transfer the tomatoes at once to a bowl of cold water. When they are cold, peel off the skins. Cut the tomatoes crosswise in half, squeeze out the seeds, then coarsely chop each half. If using canned tomatoes, chop them, reserving their juice.

2 With a chef's knife, cut the herbs into small pieces. Holding the tip of the blade against the board and rocking the knife back and forth, chop until the herbs are coarse or fine, as you wish.

ANNE SAYS
"Make sure that your knife is very sharp, otherwise you will bruise the herbs rather than cut them."

4 Put the tomatoes, with any juice, in the frying pan and add two-thirds of the garlic, the basil, and a pinch of salt.

ANNE SAYS
"*In winter months, canned tomatoes often have more flavour than fresh ones, and may be substituted for them in this dish.*"

Tomatoes are rich red in colour, indicating ripeness and flavour

Chopped fresh basil enlivens tomato sauce

Fresh garlic adds pungency to sauce

5 Cook over medium heat, stirring occasionally, until slightly thickened, 10–12 minutes; there should be some liquid left in the pan.

6 Transfer to the food processor and purée the sauce. Season to taste with salt and pepper, and set aside. Wipe the frying pan clean.

HOW TO PEEL AND CHOP GARLIC

The strength of garlic varies with its age and dryness; use more when it is very fresh.

1 To peel a garlic clove, lightly crush it with the flat side of a chef's knife to loosen the skin.

2 Peel the skin from the garlic clove with your fingers and discard. Set the flat side of the chef's knife on top of the garlic clove and strike it firmly with your fist.

3 Finely chop the garlic clove with the chef's knife, rocking the blade back and forth.

2 MAKE THE MEATBALLS

1 Strip the parsley leaves from the stalks and chop them, using the chef's knife. Put the minced beef, one-quarter of the Parmesan cheese, the chopped parsley leaves, remaining garlic, lemon juice, salt, and pepper in a bowl. Add the egg.

2 Mix all the ingredients in the bowl with your hands until they are thoroughly combined.

ANNE SAYS
"Hands make the best tools for mixing, but you can use a wooden spoon."

3 Test the mixture for seasoning: heat 15 ml (1 tbsp) oil in the frying pan, add a small spoonful of meatball mixture, and fry until brown on both sides. Taste, and adjust the seasoning of the remaining mixture, if necessary.

4 Shape the mixture into meatballs about 2 cm (3/4 inch) in diameter, wetting the palms of your hands so shaping the meat mixture is easier.

5 Heat the remaining oil in the frying pan. Add the meatballs, making sure they are not crowded in the pan. If necessary, fry them in batches.

6 Fry the meatballs briskly, turning them with the palette knife, until they are brown on the outside and still pink inside, 2–4 minutes. Transfer them to a large plate with the slotted spoon, and set aside.

! TAKE CARE !
If the oil is not hot enough, the meatballs will stick.

Turn meatballs when browned on one side

3 COOK, ASSEMBLE, AND BAKE THE RIGATONI

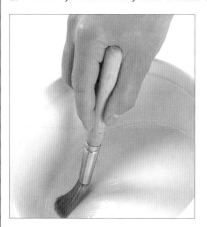

1 Heat the oven to 190°C (375°F, Gas 5). Brush the inside of the soufflé dish lightly with a little olive oil.

2 Fill a large saucepan with water, bring to a boil, and add 15 ml (1 tbsp) salt. Add the pasta to the pan and simmer until *al dente*, tender but still chewy, 8–10 minutes, or according to package directions. Stir the pasta occasionally to keep from sticking.

Rinse pasta with hot water so starch is washed away and pasta remains hot

3 Drain the pasta in the colander, rinse with hot water, and drain again thoroughly.

ANNE SAYS
"Rinsing washes away excess starch."

Shake colander while rinsing so water drains away completely

Stir gently so pasta does not break up

4 Return the rinsed and drained pasta to the saucepan and pour in the tomato-basil sauce.

5 Gently stir the pasta and sauce together until the pasta is well coated with the sauce.

6 Spoon about one-third of the pasta and sauce into the prepared soufflé dish and level the surface.

7 Spoon half of the meatballs on top. Sprinkle with one-third of the remaining Parmesan cheese. Top with half of the remaining pasta then the rest of the meatballs. Sprinkle with half of the remaining Parmesan.

Meatballs are well browned, and drained of any excess oil

8 Add the remaining pasta and cover it with the rest of the Parmesan cheese. Bake the timballo in the heated oven until very hot and the top is browned, 30–40 minutes. Let stand so the flavours blend together, about 15 minutes.

🍽 TO SERVE
Sprinkle with a little shredded basil, if you like, and serve warm.

Plump rigatoni
hides a surprise layer of meatballs underneath

Shreds of basil
hint at flavour in tomato sauce

Parmesan cheese
makes golden topping for timballo

V A R I A T I O N

BAKED ZITI WITH MOZZARELLA AND OLIVES

In this variation of baked rigatoni, Timballo di Ziti, chunks of mozzarella cheese and black olives replace the meatballs, and anchovies spice the tomato sauce.

1 Chop 8 anchovy fillets. Make the tomato sauce as directed in the main recipe, adding the chopped anchovies to the tomatoes with the garlic. Omit the basil.
2 Omit the meatballs. Stone 195 g (6 1/2 oz) oil-cured black olives. Cut 250 g (8 oz) mozzarella cheese into small cubes. Oil the soufflé dish.
3 Cook 375 g (12 oz) ziti as for the pasta in the main recipe, and drain thoroughly.
4 Layer the pasta, sauce, and fillings as directed, with the olives in place of the meatballs and the mozzarella cubes in place of the Parmesan.
5 Bake as directed until very hot and the cheese is melted, 20–25 minutes.

FRESH POLENTA WITH VEGETABLE STEW

Polenta con Fricandò

¡◎¡ SERVES 6–8 ⌣ WORK TIME 35–40 MINUTES ≋ COOKING TIME 35–50 MINUTES

EQUIPMENT

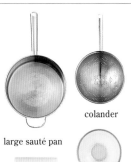

colander

large sauté pan

bowl

paper towels

saucepans

wooden spoon

whisk

slotted spoon

chef's knife

chopping board

small knife

In Italy, this creamy polenta topped with a stew of aubergines, courgettes, peppers, tomatoes, and onions would be served at the start of a meal, but it is substantial enough to act as a vegetarian main course, accompanied by a green salad.

GETTING AHEAD

The vegetable stew can be made up to 1 day ahead and refrigerated; the flavour will mellow. Reheat the stew on top of the stove and cook the polenta just before serving.

metric	SHOPPING LIST	imperial
2 litres	water	3½ pints
15 ml	salt	1 tbsp
450 g	fine cornmeal	15 oz
45 g	butter	1½ oz
	For the vegetable stew	
2	medium aubergines, total weight about 500 g (1 lb)	2
2	medium courgettes, total weight about 500 g (1 lb)	2
	salt and pepper	
3	onions	3
4	garlic cloves	4
2	red peppers	2
500 g	fresh plum tomatoes	1 lb
1	medium bunch of fresh basil	1
60 ml	olive oil, more if needed	4 tbsp

INGREDIENTS

courgettes

fine cornmeal

red peppers

aubergines

butter

onions

garlic cloves

plum tomatoes†

olive oil

fresh basil

†medium tomatoes or 425 g (14 oz) canned plum tomatoes can also be used

ORDER OF WORK

1 PREPARE THE VEGETABLES

2 COOK THE VEGETABLE STEW

3 COOK THE POLENTA

1 PREPARE THE VEGETABLES

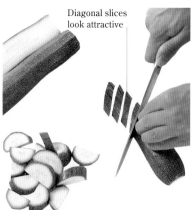

Diagonal slices look attractive

1 Trim the ends of the aubergines and cut lengthwise in half, then cut each half into 6–7 lengthwise strips. Bunch the strips together and cut them across into 2.5 cm (1 inch) chunks.

2 Trim the courgettes and cut them lengthwise in half. Cut each half diagonally into 1.25 cm (½ inch) slices.

3 Put the aubergines and courgettes on a large plate or tray and sprinkle them generously with salt. Let stand to draw out the bitter juices, 30 minutes.

When slicing, guide knife blade with curled fingers of other hand

4 Meanwhile, peel the onions, leaving a little of the root attached, and cut lengthwise in half. Lay each half flat and cut across into medium slices. Set the flat side of the chef's knife on top of each garlic clove and strike it with your fist. Discard the skins and finely chop the garlic.

5 With the small knife, cut around the pepper cores, twist, and pull them out. Halve the peppers and scrape out the seeds. Cut away the white ribs on the inside. Set each pepper half cut-side down, flatten with the heel of your hand, and slice lengthwise into strips.

6 Peel, seed, and coarsely chop the fresh tomatoes (see box, page 48). If using canned tomatoes, drain them, reserving the juice, and chop them. Strip the basil leaves from the stalks, reserving 6–8 sprigs for decoration, and pile them on the chopping board. With the chef's knife, coarsely chop the basil leaves.

7 Rinse the aubergines and courgettes with cold water and pat dry with paper towels.

2 COOK THE VEGETABLE STEW

Scatter courgette slices into pan

1 Heat 60 ml (4 tbsp) olive oil in the sauté pan. Add the onions and garlic, and cook, stirring, until soft but not brown, 3–5 minutes. Stir in the pepper slices and then the aubergine chunks, and cook 2–3 minutes longer.

2 Add the courgettes and continue cooking, stirring often, until the vegetables are just tender, 7–10 minutes. Add more oil if needed. Stir in the tomatoes with any juice, salt, and pepper. Simmer, stirring occasionally, until thickened, 12–15 minutes.

HOW TO PEEL, SEED, AND CHOP TOMATOES

Tomatoes are often peeled and seeded before they are chopped so they can be cooked to a purée. The technique is the same for plum or other tomatoes.

1 Cut the cores from the tomatoes and score an "x" on the base of each tomato with the tip of a small knife.

2 Immerse the tomatoes in a pan of boiling water until the skins start to split, 8–15 seconds, depending on their ripeness. Using a slotted spoon, transfer the tomatoes at once to a bowl of cold water.

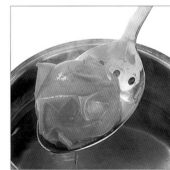

3 When the tomatoes are cool enough to handle, peel the skin off each one, using the small knife.

4 With a chef's knife, cut the tomatoes crosswise in half. Squeeze out the seeds, then coarsely chop each half.

Hold tip of blade and rock handle up and down

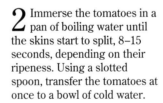

3 COOK THE POLENTA

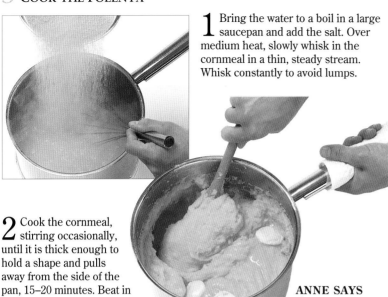

1 Bring the water to a boil in a large saucepan and add the salt. Over medium heat, slowly whisk in the cornmeal in a thin, steady stream. Whisk constantly to avoid lumps.

2 Cook the cornmeal, stirring occasionally, until it is thick enough to hold a shape and pulls away from the side of the pan, 15–20 minutes. Beat in the butter.

ANNE SAYS
"Taste the polenta; when done it should be just firm enough to hold a shape, with no taste of uncooked cornmeal."

🍴 TO SERVE

If necessary, reheat the vegetable stew. Stir in most of the chopped basil and taste for seasoning. Spoon the polenta onto warmed plates, top with stew, and sprinkle with the remaining chopped basil. Decorate with the reserved basil sprigs.

Basil sprig is bright, aromatic decoration

Red peppers accent vegetable stew

V A R I A T I O N

BARBECUED POLENTA WITH VEGETABLE STEW

Here polenta squares,
Quadrati di Polenta, *are cooked on the barbecue.*

1 Prepare the polenta as directed in the main recipe, omitting the butter.
2 Sprinkle a baking sheet with water. With a palette knife, spread the polenta evenly on the baking sheet in a 1.25 cm (¹/₂ inch) layer and cool completely.
3 Prepare the vegetable stew as directed, substituting 1 yellow, 1 green, and 1 red pepper for the 2 red peppers.
4 Heat the barbecue. Add salt and pepper to 60 ml (4 tbsp) olive oil.
5 Cut the polenta into sixteen 7.5 cm (3 inch) squares. Brush with the seasoned oil. Set the squares, oiled-side down, on the rack, and cook 10 cm (4 inches) from the heat until the rack marks show, 2–3 minutes. Rotate the squares 45° and continue cooking so the marks form diamonds. Turn over and cook on the other side. Brush with oil during and after cooking.
6 Serve the polenta squares with the vegetable stew on warmed individual plates, sprinkled with chopped basil.

ANNE SAYS
"If you don't have a barbecue, you can also fry the polenta squares in the seasoned oil: heat the oil in a large frying pan. Add the squares in batches and fry until golden, 2–3 minutes on each side, adding more oil as necessary."

SPINACH AND POTATO GNOCCHI IN TOMATO-CREAM SAUCE

Gnocchi Verdi al Sugo di Pomodoro e Panna

🍲 SERVES 6–8 🥄 WORK TIME 50–55 MINUTES ☕ COOKING TIME 30–40 MINUTES

EQUIPMENT

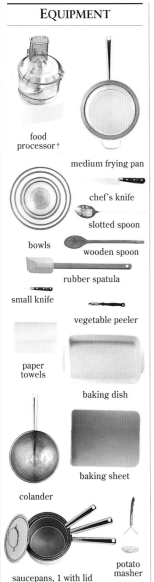

food processor†

medium frying pan

chef's knife

slotted spoon

bowls

wooden spoon

rubber spatula

small knife

vegetable peeler

paper towels

baking dish

baking sheet

colander

saucepans, 1 with lid

potato masher

†blender can also be used

I find that dumplings made only with flour can be heavy, but potato gnocchi never fail to please. Hearty, but not leaden, they are flavoured here with spinach, and served in a fresh tomato and cream sauce. The shape of the gnocchi ensures that they cook evenly and hold the sauce well.

GETTING AHEAD

The gnocchi and tomato-cream sauce can both be made up to 1 day ahead and kept separately, tightly covered, in the refrigerator. Add the cream to the sauce and bake the gnocchi just before serving.

INGREDIENTS

plum tomatoes†

baking potatoes

fresh spinach

onion

carrot

celery

butter

ground nutmeg

plain flour

double cream

†medium tomatoes or 840 g (28 oz) canned plum tomatoes can also be used

ORDER OF WORK

1 MAKE THE TOMATO-CREAM SAUCE

2 MAKE THE SPINACH AND POTATO GNOCCHI

3 COOK AND FINISH THE GNOCCHI

metric	SHOPPING LIST	imperial
1 kg	baking potatoes	2 lb
250 g	fresh or 150 g (5 oz) defrosted spinach	8 oz
125 g	plain flour, more if needed	4 oz
	For the tomato-cream sauce	
1	small onion	1
1	medium carrot	1
1	celery stick	1
1.4 kg	fresh plum tomatoes	3 lb
45 g	butter, more for baking dish	1½ oz
	salt and pepper	
250 ml	double cream	8 fl oz
1	pinch of ground nutmeg	1

1 MAKE THE TOMATO-CREAM SAUCE

Guide blade with your knuckles

1 Peel the onion, leaving a little of the root attached, and cut it lengthwise in half. Lay each half flat on a chopping board and slice horizontally toward the root, leaving the slices attached at the root end, and then slice vertically, again leaving the root end uncut. Cut across to make dice.

2 Peel and trim the carrot, cut it crosswise in half, then cut it vertically into 5 mm (1/4 inch) slices. Stack the slices and cut them into 5 mm (1/4 inch) strips. Gather the strips together and cut them crosswise to produce dice.

3 Cut the celery stick lengthwise into 5 mm (1/4 inch) strips, then gather the strips together in a pile and cut crosswise to make small dice.

ANNE SAYS
"You can chop all the vegetables together in the food processor."

4 Cut the cores from fresh tomatoes and score an "x" on the base of each with the tip of a knife. Immerse the tomatoes in a large saucepan of boiling water until the skins start to split, 8–15 seconds, depending on their ripeness. Using the slotted spoon, transfer them at once to a bowl of cold water. When cold, peel off the skins.

Remove tomatoes from boiling water as soon as skins start to split so they do not cook

Tomatoes immersed in cold water will quickly become cool enough to handle

5 Cut the tomatoes crosswise in half, squeeze out the seeds, and chop coarsely. If using canned tomatoes, chop them, reserving the juice.

6 Melt the butter in the frying pan. Add the chopped onion, carrot, and celery, and cook over medium heat, stirring, until tender, 7–10 minutes.

7 Add the tomatoes to the pan with any juice, salt, and pepper, and simmer, stirring occasionally, until thick, 25–35 minutes. Meanwhile, make the gnocchi.

8 Transfer the tomato sauce to the food processor and purée until smooth. Alternatively, work it through a sieve. Wipe the frying pan clean.

Most, but not all, liquid should have evaporated from tomato mixture

MAKE THE SPINACH AND POTATO GNOCCHI

1 Peel the potatoes and cut each one into several pieces. Put them in a medium saucepan of cold salted water, cover, and bring to a boil.

2 Simmer the potatoes until very tender when pierced with the tip of the small knife, 15–20 minutes. Drain the potatoes – they must be very dry.

ANNE SAYS
"If the potatoes seem moist, spread them on a baking sheet and let dry in a low oven with the door open, 5–10 minutes."

3 Mash the dry potatoes in the pan with the potato masher until there are no lumps remaining.

Add spinach
to pan in
handfuls

Cook spinach in boiling
water to preserve colour
and nutrients

4 Prepare the fresh spinach, if using: discard the tough ribs and stalks from the spinach, then wash the leaves under cold water.

5 Bring another saucepan of cold salted water to a boil. Add the spinach and simmer until tender, 1–2 minutes. Drain the spinach in the colander, rinse with cold water, and drain again.

Squeezing
spinach in
your fist is
best way to
remove
excess
water

6 Squeeze the cooked fresh spinach, or defrosted spinach, in your fist to remove all excess water. Purée the spinach in the food processor, or chop finely.

7 Add the spinach to the mashed potatoes with the flour, salt, and pepper, and mix together well with the wooden spoon. Taste for seasoning.

8 Transfer to a lightly floured work surface and knead lightly to form a dough, working in a little more flour to bind the mixture, if necessary.

9 To test the consistency, roll a 2 cm (³/₄ inch) ball of dough, drop it into a saucepan of simmering water, and cook until it floats to the surface. If the gnocchi falls apart, add about 30 ml (2 tbsp) more flour to the dough, then test again. If the gnocchi does not fall apart, shape the remaining dough.

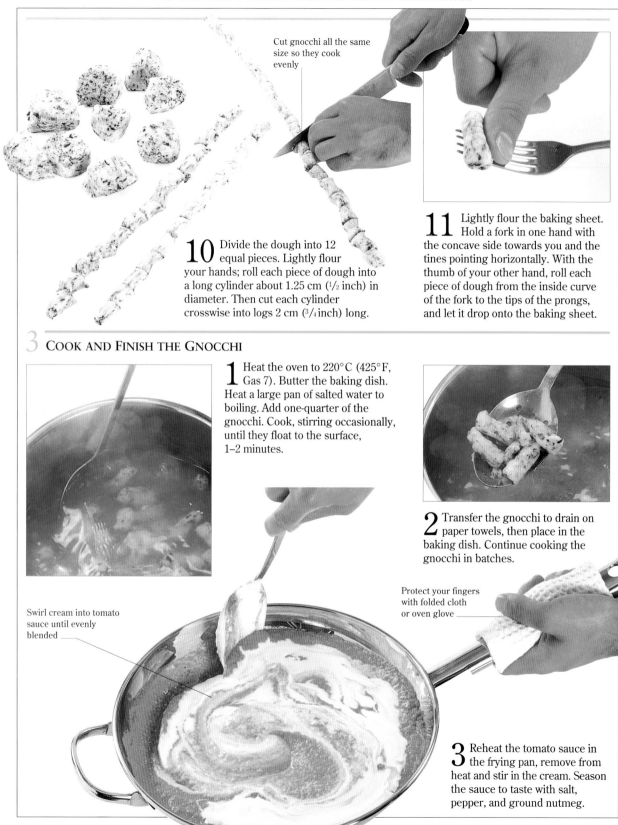

Cut gnocchi all the same
size so they cook
evenly

10 Divide the dough into 12
equal pieces. Lightly flour
your hands; roll each piece of dough into
a long cylinder about 1.25 cm (½ inch) in
diameter. Then cut each cylinder
crosswise into logs 2 cm (¾ inch) long.

11 Lightly flour the baking sheet.
Hold a fork in one hand with
the concave side towards you and the
tines pointing horizontally. With the
thumb of your other hand, roll each
piece of dough from the inside curve
of the fork to the tips of the prongs,
and let it drop onto the baking sheet.

3 COOK AND FINISH THE GNOCCHI

1 Heat the oven to 220°C (425°F,
Gas 7). Butter the baking dish.
Heat a large pan of salted water to
boiling. Add one-quarter of the
gnocchi. Cook, stirring occasionally,
until they float to the surface,
1–2 minutes.

2 Transfer the gnocchi to drain on
paper towels, then place in the
baking dish. Continue cooking the
gnocchi in batches.

Swirl cream into tomato
sauce until evenly
blended

Protect your fingers
with folded cloth
or oven glove

3 Reheat the tomato sauce in
the frying pan, remove from
heat and stir in the cream. Season
the sauce to taste with salt,
pepper, and ground nutmeg.

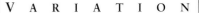

Coat gnocchi completely with sauce so they do not dry out during baking

4 Spoon the sauce evenly over the gnocchi in the baking dish. Bake the gnocchi in the heated oven until very hot and starting to brown, 5–7 minutes. Serve immediately, sprinkled with chopped flat-leaf parsley if you like.

Tomato-cream sauce makes a colourful contrast to spinach gnocchi

Chopped parsley is sprinkled over sauce before serving

V A R I A T I O N
SPINACH AND POTATO GNOCCHI WITH CHEESE

1 Omit the tomato-cream sauce. Make and cook the spinach gnocchi, and heat the oven as directed in the main recipe.
2 Arrange half of the gnocchi in a single layer on the bottom of a buttered large baking dish.
3 Thinly slice 250 g (8 oz) fontina, Gruyère, or mozzarella cheese; melt 60 g (2 oz) butter. Top the gnocchi with half of the cheese; spoon on half of the butter. Season with salt and pepper.
4 Spread the gnocchi on top, then the remaining cheese and melted butter. Season again.
5 Bake until the cheese is melted and the gnocchi are very hot, 7–10 minutes. Serve immediately.

V A R I A T I O N
PLAIN GNOCCHI WITH GORGONZOLA SAUCE

A thyme-scented, creamy Gorgonzola sauce tops plain gnocchi here.

1 Make plain gnocchi as directed in the main recipe, omitting the spinach and using 100 g (3³/₄ oz) flour for the dough. Cover the gnocchi and keep them warm in a low oven.
2 Omit the tomato-cream sauce and make a Gorgonzola sauce: cut 175 g (6 oz) Gorgonzola or other blue cheese into small cubes.
3 Strip the leaves from 10–12 sprigs of fresh thyme and pile them on a chopping board. With a chef's knife, finely chop the leaves.
4 Melt 45 g (1¹/₂ oz) butter in a large saucepan and stir in 175 ml (6 fl oz) double cream. Add the Gorgonzola, chopped thyme, salt, and pepper, and heat gently, stirring, until the cheese is melted. Do not let boil.
5 Add the sauce to the gnocchi and taste for seasoning.
6 Spoon the gnocchi with Gorgonzola sauce onto warmed individual plates and decorate with a thyme sprig. Sprinkle with 30 g (1 oz) freshly grated Parmesan cheese, if you like.

SOLE FILLETS MARINATED IN WINE VINEGAR

Sfogi in Saor

🍽 SERVES 4–6　🥣 WORK TIME 30–35 MINUTES*　🍲 COOKING TIME 6–8 MINUTES

EQUIPMENT

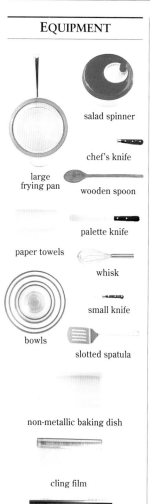

salad spinner

chef's knife

large frying pan

wooden spoon

palette knife

paper towels

whisk

small knife

bowls

slotted spatula

non-metallic baking dish

cling film

aluminium foil

chopping board

Before the days of refrigeration, pickling was a common method of preserving. This delicious sole recipe has survived despite modern appliances. The quantity given here serves 4 as a main course, 6 as an appetizer.

GETTING AHEAD

The fish can be cooked and covered with the marinade up to 1 day ahead. Keep it, tightly covered, in the refrigerator.

*plus 12–24 hours marinating time

INGREDIENTS

sole fillets

red wine vinegar

rocket

raisins

plain flour

orange juice

onion

olive oil

pine nuts

ANNE SAYS

"If you prefer a milder marinade, use half of the quantity of vinegar and an equal amount of white wine."

ORDER OF WORK

1　PREPARE THE MARINADE

2　COOK AND MARINATE THE FISH

3　PREPARE THE SALAD AND SERVE THE SOLE

metric	SHOPPING LIST	imperial
1	large onion	1
90 ml	olive oil	3 1/2 fl oz
	salt and pepper	
250 ml	red wine vinegar	8 fl oz
45 g	raisins	1 1/2 oz
500 g	sole fillets	1 lb
30 g	plain flour	1 oz
30 g	pine nuts	1 oz
	For the salad	
250 g	rocket	8 oz
	juice of 1/2 orange	
45 ml	olive oil	3 tbsp

1 PREPARE THE MARINADE

1 Peel the onion, leaving a little of the root attached, and cut lengthwise in half through root and stalk.

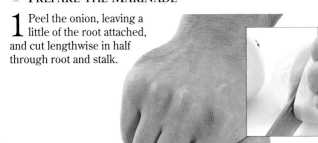

Small knife makes peeling easy

ANNE SAYS
"Onions should be firm, with no sign of sprouting, and no black or powdery spots."

2 Lay each onion half flat on the chopping board and cut across into thin slices.

3 Heat one-third of the oil in the large frying pan. Add the onion slices with a little salt and pepper, cover with foil, and cook over low heat, stirring occasionally, until very soft, 15–20 minutes.

Sweetness of raisins counterbalances sharpness of vinegar

4 Remove the foil from the frying pan, increase the heat, and continue cooking the onion slices until they are lightly browned and caramelized, 3–5 minutes.

5 Add the red wine vinegar and the raisins to the onions. Heat to boiling, and boil 2 minutes.

6 Transfer the vinegar mixture from the frying pan to a bowl; set aside while preparing the fish.

2 COOK AND MARINATE THE FISH

Sole has delicate, fine-textured flesh

Dry fish with paper towels so flour does not clog when coating

1 Rinse the sole fillets and pat dry with paper towels. With the chef's knife, cut the fillets crosswise into pieces about 5 cm (2 inches) wide.

2 Spread the flour on a large plate and season with salt and pepper. Add some of the fish pieces and, with a fork, turn the pieces in the seasoned flour so they are evenly coated. Transfer to a second plate and coat the remaining fish pieces.

ANNE SAYS
"If necessary, cook the fish in batches so the pan is not crowded, adding more oil when required."

3 Heat the remaining oil and add the sole pieces. Cook over medium-high heat until browned, 1–2 minutes.

4 Turn the sole pieces, and pan-fry until the flesh just flakes when tested with a fork, 1–2 minutes longer. Drain the fish on paper towels and let cool completely.

Test fish as soon as it loses its transparent appearance because it quickly overcooks

5 Spread the sole pieces in the baking dish and cover them with the vinegar mixture.

6 Sprinkle with the pine nuts. Cover tightly and leave to marinate in the refrigerator, 12 hours, or up to 24 hours.

PREPARE THE SALAD AND SERVE THE SOLE

1 Discard the tough stalks from the rocket and wash the leaves in plenty of cold water. Dry the leaves in the salad spinner or on a tea towel.

2 Pour the orange juice into a large bowl and whisk in salt and pepper to taste. Gradually whisk in the oil so the vinaigrette emulsifies and thickens slightly. Taste for seasoning.

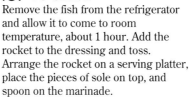

🍽 TO SERVE

Remove the fish from the refrigerator and allow it to come to room temperature, about 1 hour. Add the rocket to the dressing and toss. Arrange the rocket on a serving platter, place the pieces of sole on top, and spoon on the marinade.

Crisp, bitter rocket leaves and crunchy nuts complement sweet-and-sour fish

Small pieces of fish absorb flavour from marinade

V A R I A T I O N

SOLE FILLETS MARINATED WITH WINE VINEGAR AND SAFFRON

Saffron adds an attractive colour to the pickling liquid in Pesce a Scapece.

1 Omit the onion, raisins, and pine nuts from the main recipe. Peel and chop 2 garlic cloves: set the flat side of a chef's knife on top of each garlic clove and strike it with your fist. Discard the skins and finely chop the garlic.
2 Prepare and fry the sole pieces as directed in the main recipe, and spread them in the baking dish.
3 Put 175 ml (6 fl oz) white wine vinegar and a large pinch of saffron in a small pan. Bring to a boil, then let cool.
4 Whisk in the chopped garlic and 75 ml (2 ½ fl oz) olive oil. Pour this marinade over the sole pieces and season with plenty of black pepper. Cover tightly, and leave to marinate in the refrigerator, as directed.
5 Remove the fish from the refrigerator, and allow to come to room temperature.
6 Meanwhile, prepare the rocket and orange dressing as directed, and toss the leaves in the dressing.
7 Arrange the salad leaves on individual plates with the pieces of fish on top. Decorate with a twisted lemon slice, if you like.

ANNE SAYS

"If your vinegar is very acidic, use only 125 ml (4 fl oz) vinegar and add 60 ml (4 tbsp) water."

BEEF BRAISED IN RED WINE

Stufato di Manzo al Barbera

 SERVES 6 🥄 WORK TIME 15–20 MINUTES 🍲 COOKING TIME 4–4½ HOURS

EQUIPMENT

large flameproof casserole with lid

aluminium foil

chopping board

wooden spoons

2-pronged fork

vegetable peeler

chef's knife

small knife

ANNE SAYS
"*A thick earthenware casserole that is glazed on the inside is traditionally used because it allows the beef to cook slowly and evenly. The fragrant steam produced during cooking condenses on the lid and drips back onto the meat, basting it and keeping it moist.*"

A beef roast braised in red wine is a favourite dish in northern Italy. Ovens did not find their way into many domestic kitchens until after World War II, so Stufato *was traditionally cooked on top of the stove. Barbera is the preferred wine but you can substitute any dry red. Gnocchi (see page 50), served in the wine sauce, is the perfect accompaniment, although braised carrots or leeks are also delicious.*

GETTING AHEAD

The beef can be prepared up to 3 days ahead and kept, covered, in the refrigerator. Reheat it on top of the stove, stirring occasionally, before serving.

metric	SHOPPING LIST	imperial
1	small carrot	1
1	celery stick	1
1	small onion	1
1	rolled silverside of beef, weighing about 1.8 kg (4 lb)	1
30 ml	olive oil	2 tbsp
500 ml	dry red wine	16 fl oz
15 ml	tomato purée	1 tbsp
500 ml	beef stock (see box, page 122), more if needed	16 fl oz
2–3	sprigs of fresh thyme	2–3
	salt and pepper	

INGREDIENTS

silverside of beef

dry red wine

celery

fresh thyme

onion

tomato purée

carrot

olive oil

beef stock†

†water can also be used

ANNE SAYS
"*Barbera is the most widely produced wine of Piedmont. The best varieties will have a* Denominazione di Origine Controllate (D.O.C.), *but even these are everyday wines.*"

ORDER OF WORK

1. PREPARE THE VEGETABLES

2. COOK THE BEEF

1 PREPARE THE VEGETABLES

"Squared-off" carrot is easy to dice

1 Peel and trim the carrot. Cut it crosswise in half and square off the sides using the chef's knife. Cut the halves vertically into 5 mm (¹/₄ inch) slices. Stack the slices and cut into 5 mm (¹/₄ inch) strips. Gather the strips and cut crosswise to produce dice.

2 Peel the strings from the celery stick with the vegetable peeler. Cut in half, then cut the halves lengthwise into 5 mm (¹/₄ inch) strips. Gather the strips together in a pile and cut crosswise to make small dice. Chop the onion (see box, right).

2 COOK THE BEEF

1 Heat the oven to 150°C (300°F, Gas 2). With the chef's knife, trim any excess fat and sinew from the beef. Heat the oil in the casserole.

2 Add the beef to the casserole and brown it well on all sides, turning it with 2 wooden spoons. Transfer the beef to a plate, and set aside.

Turning with spoons stops beef from being pierced and losing juices

Hot oil sears beef, sealing in juices

HOW TO CHOP AN ONION

The size of dice when chopping an onion depends on the thickness of the initial slices. For a standard size, make slices about 5 mm (¹/₄ inch) thick. For finely chopped onions, slice as thinly as possible.

1 Peel the onion and trim the top; leave a little of the root attached. Cut the onion lengthwise in half with a chef's knife.

2 Lay each onion half, cut-side down, on a chopping board. With the chef's knife, slice the onion half horizontally towards the root, leaving the slices attached at the root end.

3 Then slice the onion vertically, again leaving the root end uncut. Finally, cut across the onion to make dice.

Wine dissolves caramelized meat juices

3 Add the onion, carrot, and celery to the casserole and cook over medium heat, stirring occasionally, until the vegetables are soft, 3–5 minutes.

4 Add the red wine to the casserole, stir to dissolve the pan juices, and bring the liquid to a boil.

5 Stir in the tomato purée until evenly blended. Return the beef to the casserole. Add enough beef stock to come halfway up the sides of the meat.

Cooking liquid should be simmering

6 Add the thyme sprigs and season with salt and pepper. Bring the liquid to a boil on top of the stove, then cover the casserole tightly.

7 Cook in the heated oven until the meat is very tender when pierced with the 2-pronged fork, 4–4^1/$_2$ hours. Turn the meat 3–4 times during cooking and add more stock if the casserole seems dry.

! TAKE CARE !
The cooking liquid should remain at a simmer, not boiling, so the beef does not cook too quickly.

Foil is excellent insulator

Cover meat with foil, shiny side outwards, to keep meat warm

8 Transfer the meat to the chopping board and cover with foil, to keep it warm. Boil the cooking liquid until thickened and reduced to about 250 ml (8 fl oz). Discard the thyme sprigs and taste the cooking liquid for seasoning.

9 Using the chef's knife, carve the meat into neat slices on the chopping board.

🍽 **TO SERVE**

Arrange the beef slices on warmed individual plates. If you like, serve the beef with gnocchi. Spoon a little cooking liquid over the beef and gnocchi and serve the rest separately.

Gnocchi is a perfect partner for beef braised in red wine

Cooking juices are dark and rich

V A R I A T I O N

BRAISED LAMB WITH POTATOES AND TOMATOES

Agnello al Forno con Patate e Pomodori – lamb braised with potatoes and tomatoes – is popular in southern Italy.

1 Trim 1 kg (2 lb) boneless leg of lamb; cut it into 4 cm (1½ inch) cubes.
2 Peel, seed, and coarsely chop 375 g (12 oz) ripe plum or medium tomatoes.
3 Chop the onion and carrot. Omit the celery. Peel 500 g (1 lb) new potatoes.
4 Substitute 125 ml (4 fl oz) dry white wine for the red, and the same amount of fresh rosemary for the thyme sprigs. Omit the tomato purée and beef stock.
5 Brown the lamb cubes in a medium flameproof casserole, then sauté the onion and carrot as directed. Add the white wine and rosemary and boil until reduced by half.
6 Return the lamb cubes to the casserole, add the chopped tomatoes, and salt and pepper. Bring to a boil, cover, and simmer 30 minutes on top of the stove. Heat the oven to 150°C (300°F, Gas 2).
7 Transfer the casserole to the oven and cook the lamb 30 minutes. Add the potatoes and continue cooking, stirring occasionally, until the lamb cubes are tender, 1¼–1¾ hours longer. Add water during cooking if the casserole becomes dry.
8 Taste the cooking liquid for seasoning. Serve hot from the casserole.

MILANESE VEAL ESCALOPES

Scaloppine alla Milanese

 SERVES 6   WORK TIME 20–25 MINUTES   FRYING TIME 4–12 MINUTES*

EQUIPMENT

shallow dish

frying pans

wooden spoon

sieve

2-pronged fork

small knife

paper towels

bowl

chef's knife

rolling pin

greaseproof paper†

chopping board

†cling film can also be used

INGREDIENTS

veal escalopes

eggs

fresh oregano

garlic clove

butter

olive oil

green pepper

lemon

red pepper

grated Parmesan cheese

plain flour

dried breadcrumbs

In this northern Italian classic, veal escalopes are coated with breadcrumbs and cheese, and lightly fried. The accompaniment of peppers sautéed in garlic and olive oil is a favourite of mine.

GETTING AHEAD

The veal escalopes can be coated up to 4 hours ahead; keep them uncovered in the refrigerator.

* total frying time depends on size of frying pan

metric	SHOPPING LIST	imperial
6	veal escalopes, total weight about 375 g (12 oz)	6
30 g	plain flour	1 oz
	salt and pepper	
2	eggs	2
60 g	dried breadcrumbs	2 oz
60 g	freshly grated Parmesan cheese	2 oz
1	lemon for garnish	1
30 g	butter	1 oz
30 ml	olive oil, more if needed	2 tbsp
	For the sautéed peppers	
1	garlic clove	1
7–10	sprigs of fresh oregano	7-10
1	small green pepper	1
1	small red pepper	1
30 ml	olive oil	2 tbsp

ORDER OF WORK

1 PREPARE THE VEAL ESCALOPES

2 SAUTE THE PEPPERS

3 MAKE THE GARNISH AND FRY THE VEAL

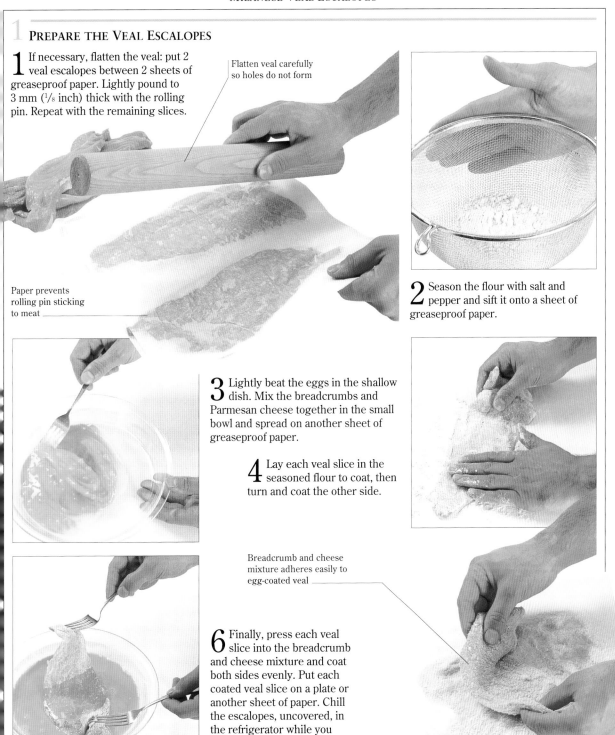

1 PREPARE THE VEAL ESCALOPES

1 If necessary, flatten the veal: put 2 veal escalopes between 2 sheets of greaseproof paper. Lightly pound to 3 mm (¹/₈ inch) thick with the rolling pin. Repeat with the remaining slices.

Flatten veal carefully so holes do not form

Paper prevents rolling pin sticking to meat

2 Season the flour with salt and pepper and sift it onto a sheet of greaseproof paper.

3 Lightly beat the eggs in the shallow dish. Mix the breadcrumbs and Parmesan cheese together in the small bowl and spread on another sheet of greaseproof paper.

4 Lay each veal slice in the seasoned flour to coat, then turn and coat the other side.

Breadcrumb and cheese mixture adheres easily to egg-coated veal

6 Finally, press each veal slice into the breadcrumb and cheese mixture and coat both sides evenly. Put each coated veal slice on a plate or another sheet of paper. Chill the escalopes, uncovered, in the refrigerator while you sauté the peppers.

ANNE SAYS
"*Coating will dry and be extra crisp if escalopes are chilled 1–4 hours before frying.*"

5 Using 2 forks, dip each floured veal slice in the beaten egg and coat it thoroughly on both sides.

2 SAUTE THE PEPPERS

1 Set the flat side of the chef's knife on top of the garlic clove and strike it with your fist. Discard the skin and finely chop the garlic. Strip the oregano leaves from the stalks, reserving 6 of the top sprigs for garnish. Finely chop the leaves with the chef's knife.

2 Cut around the core of each pepper and pull it out. Halve each pepper lengthwise and scrape out the seeds. Cut away the white ribs on the inside.

Add pepper strips to frying pan all at once

3 Set each pepper half cut-side down on the work surface, flatten it with the heel of your hand, and slice it lengthwise into thin strips.

When pepper strips are sliced thinly they will soften quickly in hot oil

4 Heat the oil in a medium frying pan. Add the garlic, pepper strips, salt, and pepper, and sauté, stirring occasionally, until softened, 7–10 minutes. Remove from the heat, add the chopped oregano, and taste for seasoning; keep warm while frying the escalopes.

3 MAKE THE GARNISH AND FRY THE VEAL

2 Add 2–3 escalopes to the pan and fry over medium-high heat until golden brown, 1–2 minutes.

ANNE SAYS
"*The escalopes should not touch or they will stick together.*"

Cook escalopes in batches to avoid crowding in pan

1 Slice the lemon for the garnish; set aside. Heat half of the butter and 15 ml (1 tbsp) oil in a large frying pan.

If coating catches, wipe out pan and add more oil between batches

3 Turn the escalopes with the 2-pronged fork, and continue cooking until brown on the outside and no longer pink in the centre, about 1–2 minutes. Transfer to a plate lined with paper towels and keep warm. Add the remaining butter and oil to the pan and fry the remaining veal, adding more oil to the pan if necessary.

🍽 TO SERVE

Transfer the escalopes to warmed individual plates and garnish each with a lemon slice and a sprig of oregano. Spoon the pepper strips alongside.

Coating is crisp and golden brown

Pepper strips make bright colour contrast

V A R I A T I O N

VEAL ESCALOPES WITH PARMA HAM

Escalopes topped with Parma ham and cheese are baked until the cheese melts to form Scaloppine alla Modenese.

1 Coat the veal escalopes as directed in the main recipe, omitting the Parmesan cheese and using double the amount of breadcrumbs.
2 Grate 125 g (4 oz) fontina or Gruyère cheese. Trim the fat from 6 thin slices of Parma ham (total weight about 75 g/2¹/₂ oz) so they are smaller than the veal escalopes.
3 Omit the green pepper. Cut the red pepper into strips as directed in the main recipe. Peel 1 onion, leaving a little of the root attached, and cut lengthwise in half. Cut across into thin slices. Heat 30 ml (2 tbsp) olive oil in a frying pan, add the onion and sauté until soft, 2–3 minutes. Add the pepper and continue sautéing as directed in the main recipe.
4 Heat the oven to 200°C (400°F, Gas 6). Fry the escalopes as directed.
5 Put the cooked escalopes on a baking sheet. Lay a slice of Parma ham on each slice of veal and sprinkle with the grated cheese.
6 Bake the escalopes in the heated oven until the cheese topping is melted and bubbling, 5–7 minutes.
7 Serve on warmed individual plates with wedges of lemon. If you like, garnish each escalope with a sprig of flat-leaf parsley.

SAUTEED LIVER AND ONIONS

Fegato alla Veneziana

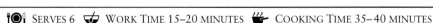

🍽 SERVES 6 🥣 WORK TIME 15–20 MINUTES 🍲 COOKING TIME 35–40 MINUTES

EQUIPMENT

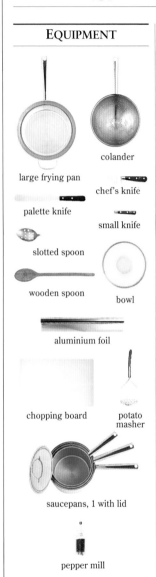

colander

large frying pan

chef's knife

palette knife

small knife

slotted spoon

wooden spoon

bowl

aluminium foil

chopping board

potato masher

saucepans, 1 with lid

pepper mill

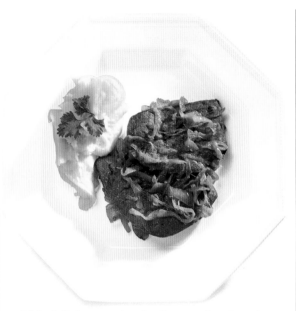

This delicious recipe for liver and onions is a classic Venetian dish, which is now found throughout Italy. Very thin slices of calf's liver are quickly sautéed in olive oil and served with meltingly soft caramelized onions and buttery mashed potatoes.

GETTING AHEAD

The onions can be sautéed up to 8 hours ahead and reheated; make sure you leave the oil in the frying pan. Prepare the mashed potatoes and sauté the liver just before serving.

INGREDIENTS

onions

calf's liver

butter

olive oil

potatoes

black peppercorns

milk

ANNE SAYS

"Try to find calf's liver in one piece so that you can cut it into the thinnest possible slices yourself, rather than buying it pre-sliced by your butcher."

ORDER OF WORK

1 PREPARE THE ONIONS

2 PREPARE THE MASHED POTATOES

3 PREPARE THE LIVER

metric	SHOPPING LIST	imperial
1 kg	large onions	2 lb
90 ml	olive oil	3 fl oz
	salt and freshly ground black pepper	
750 g	calf's liver	1½ lb
	For the mashed potatoes	
635 g	potatoes	1¼ lb
60 ml	milk	4 tbsp
60 g	butter	2 oz

1 PREPARE THE ONIONS

1 Slice the onions (see box, below). Heat two-thirds of the oil in the frying pan. Add the onions with a little salt and pepper, and cover with foil.

2 Cook the onions over low heat, stirring occasionally, until very soft, 25–30 minutes. Meanwhile, prepare the mashed potatoes (see page 70).

Stir onions to prevent sticking

Slow cooking develops sweetness of onions

3 Remove the foil from the onions, increase the heat to medium-high, and cook, stirring constantly, until the onions are golden brown and caramelized, 5–7 minutes longer.

Stir onions so they caramelize evenly

! TAKE CARE !
Do not let the onions catch on the bottom of the pan or they will taste bitter.

4 Transfer the onions to the bowl with the slotted spoon, leaving any excess oil in the pan to sauté the liver.

HOW TO SLICE AN ONION

Onions are often sliced for soups and stews, as well as for sautéing. The root is left on for slicing, to help hold the onion together.

1 Peel the onion and trim the top, leaving a little of the root attached. Cut the onion lengthwise in half.

2 Put one half, cut-side down, on a chopping board. Holding the onion firmly, slice it crosswise, guiding the knife with bent fingers. Discard the root. Repeat with the other onion half.

Use your knuckles to guide blade of knife

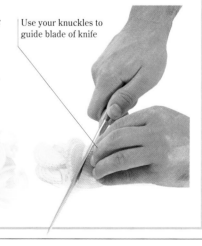

2 PREPARE THE MASHED POTATOES

1 Wash and peel the potatoes and cut them into pieces. Bring a medium saucepan of salted water to a boil. Add the potatoes, cover, and cook until tender when pierced with the small knife, 15–20 minutes.

2 Drain the potatoes thoroughly. Return them to the pan and mash them with the potato masher. Heat the milk in a small saucepan. Add the butter, salt, and pepper, and beat until mixed. Gradually add the hot milk to the potatoes, beating constantly until the potatoes are light and fluffy, about 5 minutes. Taste for seasoning and keep warm.

Butter will melt into milk

3 PREPARE THE LIVER

1 Peel any skin from the liver. Cut off any exposed ducts or connective tissue. Cut the liver into slices, about 5 mm (¼ inch) thick. If more than 7.5 cm (3 inches) long, cut them in half.

Sharp chef's knife cuts liver cleanly and does not tear fibres

2 Remove any internal ducts, and season the liver with salt and freshly ground pepper.

ANNE SAYS
"Season the liver just before frying because salt draws out the juices."

Thin, uniform slices of meat will cook quickly and evenly

3 Add the remaining oil to the frying pan and heat the oil over high heat. Add half of the liver and cook just until browned, 45–60 seconds.

4 Turn the slices with the palette knife and brown the other side, 45–60 seconds.

5 The slices should cook very quickly in a single layer without overlapping, so they are browned on the outside but still pink in the centre.

ANNE SAYS
"Liver should always be pink in the centre. Do not overcook it or it will be tough."

6 Transfer the liver to a plate and keep warm. Cook the remaining liver in the same way.

7 Return the onions to the pan with all of the liver and stir quickly over high heat until very hot, 30–60 seconds. Season with salt and pepper.

Liver and onions are reheated quickly together

🍽 TO SERVE
Reheat the mashed potatoes if necessary. Transfer liver and onions to warmed individual plates, and serve at once, with the potatoes.

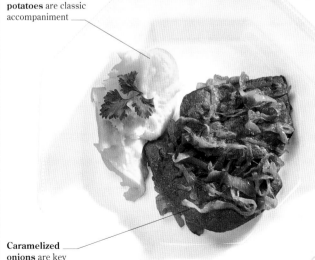

Creamy mashed potatoes are classic accompaniment

Caramelized onions are key ingredient

SAUTEED LIVER WITH WINE VINEGAR

Fegato all'Aceto is a tangy variation of Sautéed Liver and Onions.

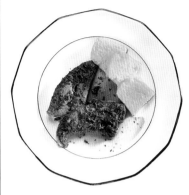

1 Omit the onions. Strip the leaves from 1 medium bunch of flat-leaf or curly parsley and pile them on a chopping board. Finely chop the leaves, using a chef's knife. Cut the liver into thin slices as directed in the main recipe.
2 Heat 30 ml (2 tbsp) oil and 30 g (1 oz) butter in a large frying pan over high heat. Cook half of the liver as directed until browned on both sides but still slightly pink in the centre.
3 Cook the remaining liver in the same way, keeping the first batch warm.
4 Reduce the heat to medium, return the first batch of liver to the pan; pour over 60 ml (4 tbsp) red wine vinegar. Sprinkle with the parsley, season with salt and pepper, and stir to mix.
5 Serve on warmed individual plates, accompanied by slices of fried polenta, if you like.

DEVILLED CHICKEN

Pollo alla Diavola

 SERVES 4   WORK TIME 20–25 MINUTES*   COOKING TIME 35–50 MINUTES

EQUIPMENT

large non-metallic baking dish

whisk

lemon squeezer

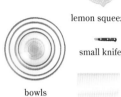

small knife

bowls

paper towels

chef's knife

2-pronged fork

pepper mill

poultry shears

pastry brush   rubber gloves

2 long metal skewers

chopping board

ANNE SAYS

"Devilled chicken is ideally suited to barbecuing. In this case, bake the tomatoes separately in a baking dish. Spoon the crumb-herb mixture on them, and bake in a 200°C (400°F, Gas 6) oven, 10–12 minutes."

Fresh chillies give this hot chicken dish its name. The backbone is removed from the chicken, which is then flattened and marinated in lemon juice, red chillies, and freshly ground black pepper. Tomatoes topped with garlic, parsley, and olive oil are grilled with the chicken to serve as an accompaniment.

--- GETTING AHEAD ---

The chicken can be marinated up to 1 day ahead – it will be spicier. Grill it with the tomatoes just before serving.

*plus 8 hours marinating time

metric	SHOPPING LIST	imperial
1	small chicken, weighing about 1.4 kg (3 lb)	1
4	lemons	4
2	fresh red chillies	2
30 ml	olive oil, more for grill rack	2 tbsp
	salt and freshly ground black pepper	
	For the grilled tomatoes	
2	large tomatoes, total weight about 500 g (1 lb)	2
5–7	sprigs of flat-leaf parsley	5–7
2	garlic cloves	2
30 g	dried breadcrumbs	1 oz
15 ml	olive oil	1 tbsp

INGREDIENTS

chicken

lemons

fresh red chillies†

tomatoes

garlic cloves

flat-leaf parsley‡

dried breadcrumbs

black peppercorns

olive oil

†dried red chillies can also be used
‡curly parsley can also be used

ORDER OF WORK

1 SPLIT AND FLATTEN THE CHICKEN

2 MARINATE THE CHICKEN

3 PREPARE THE TOMATOES

4 GRILL THE CHICKEN AND TOMATOES

1 SPLIT AND FLATTEN THE CHICKEN

1 Set the chicken breast-side down on the chopping board. With the poultry shears, cut along each side of the backbone.

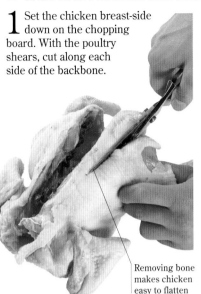

Removing bone makes chicken easy to flatten

2 Discard the backbone from the chicken and, using the chef's knife, trim off any flaps of skin.

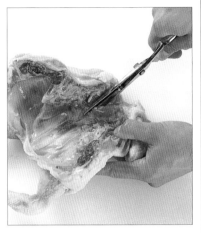

3 Force the bird open and, with the poultry shears, snip the wishbone. Wipe the bird inside and outside with paper towels.

4 Turn the bird breast-side up, cut off the wing tips, and discard them. Turn the legs inwards.

Use both hands to break breastbone of chicken

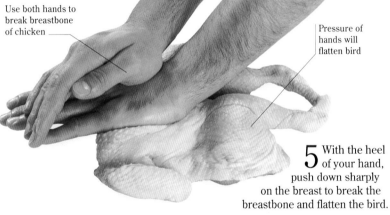

Pressure of hands will flatten bird

5 With the heel of your hand, push down sharply on the breast to break the breastbone and flatten the bird.

Chicken legs are secured by tucking into slits in skin

6 Using the small knife, make a small cut in the skin between the leg and breastbone and tuck in the end of the leg.

7 Holding the legs carefully in position, set the flattened chicken in the large baking dish.

2 MARINATE THE CHICKEN

1 Squeeze the juice from 3 of the lemons – there should be about 125 ml (4 fl oz) juice. Core, seed, and dice the fresh chillies (see box, below). Chop dried chillies, if using.

2 Whisk the lemon juice, diced chillies, oil, and 10 ml (2 tsp) freshly ground black pepper in a bowl until thoroughly mixed.

3 Pour the marinade over the chicken. Cover and leave to marinate in the refrigerator 8 hours or overnight, turning and basting the chicken occasionally.

HOW TO CORE, SEED, AND DICE FRESH CHILLIES

Fresh chillies must be finely chopped so their heat is spread evenly through the dish. For a hotter flavour, you can add the seeds too. Chillies can burn your skin, so be sure to wear rubber gloves, and to avoid contact with your eyes.

Remove all seeds unless very hot flavour is wanted

1 Cut the chillies lengthwise in half with a small knife. Cut out the core and fleshy white ribs and scrape out the seeds.

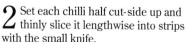

2 Set each chilli half cut-side up and thinly slice it lengthwise into strips with the small knife.

3 Gather the chilli strips together with your fingers and cut them across to produce very fine dice.

3 PREPARE THE TOMATOES

Tomato halves are ready for crumb-herb topping

1 Cut the cores from the tomatoes. Cut the tomatoes horizontally in half with the chef's knife.

2 If necessary, cut a small slice off the base of each half so it will sit flat on the grill rack; set aside.

Pull leaves gently from stalks

Parsley will add colour as well as flavour to baked tomatoes

3 Strip the parsley leaves from the stalks, reserving a few sprigs for decoration. Pile the leaves on the chopping board. With the chef's knife, finely chop them.

4 Set the flat side of the chef's knife on top of each garlic clove and strike it with your fist. Discard the skins and finely chop the garlic.

5 Put the chopped parsley, garlic, breadcrumbs, and oil into a small bowl, and season generously with salt and freshly ground black pepper.

6 Stir the crumb-herb mixture thoroughly until well mixed together; set aside.

4 GRILL THE CHICKEN AND TOMATOES

Skewers keep chicken flat during cooking

First skewer is threaded through wings and breastbone

1 Heat the grill. Remove the chicken from the marinade, reserving the marinade for basting. Thread 1 skewer through the wings and breastbone of the bird to hold it flat. Thread the second skewer through the legs. Sprinkle with a little salt.

2 Brush the grill rack with oil and set the chicken on it, skin-side up. Grill the chicken about 10 cm (4 inches) from the heat, basting occasionally with the reserved marinade, until the skin is golden brown, 15–20 minutes.

Crumb-herb topping turns golden brown when grilled

3 Remove the grill pan from the heat and turn over the chicken. Set the tomato halves alongside, cut-side up. Continue grilling, basting the chicken from time to time, 10–15 minutes.

4 Turn the chicken again and spoon the crumb-herb mixture onto the tomatoes. Continue cooking, basting the chicken often, until the skin is slightly charred. The juices from the thigh should run clear when the meat is pierced, 10–15 minutes longer. The tomatoes should be tender and browned on top; if necessary, grill the tomatoes a few minutes longer.

ANNE SAYS
"If the skin of the chicken browns too quickly during grilling, turn the chicken over again and cook so the skin side is away from the heat."

5 While the chicken is cooking, cut the remaining lemon into slices; reserve the slices for decoration.

Cut chicken across so some white meat is included with leg

6 Remove the skewers from the chicken. Holding the chicken with the 2-pronged fork, split the breastbone with the chef's knife, dividing the bird in half. Cut each half across to make 4 even portions.

🍴 TO SERVE

Transfer the chicken pieces and tomato halves to warmed plates. Decorate with the reserved lemon and parsley.

Crisp chicken skin is flecked with pieces of chilli

Juicy grilled tomatoes are a foil to piquant chicken

V A R I A T I O N

GRILLED CHICKEN DRUMSTICKS WITH ROSEMARY

Gambe di Pollo ai Ferri *make delicious picnic fare. You can cook chicken wings or whole legs in the same way.*

1 Substitute 8 chicken drumsticks for the whole chicken and make a garlic-herb marinade in place of the devilled mixture: peel and finely chop 3 garlic cloves. Remove the leaves from 8–10 sprigs of fresh rosemary and finely chop the leaves.
2 Mix the garlic and rosemary with the juice of 1 lemon, 75 ml (2½ fl oz) olive oil, and black pepper to taste. Marinate the chicken as directed.
3 Remove the drumsticks from the marinade. Sprinkle them with salt, and grill or barbecue them, turning and basting occasionally, until the juices run clear when the chicken is pierced with a fork, 20–30 minutes.
4 Omit the baked tomatoes. Arrange the drumsticks on a serving platter and surround with sliced tomatoes sprinkled with a little olive oil, lemon juice, and finely chopped fresh parsley.

SPINACH-STUFFED VEAL ROLLS

Messicani di Vitello

🍽 SERVES 4   🥄 WORK TIME 45–50 MINUTES   🍲 COOKING TIME 30–40 MINUTES

EQUIPMENT

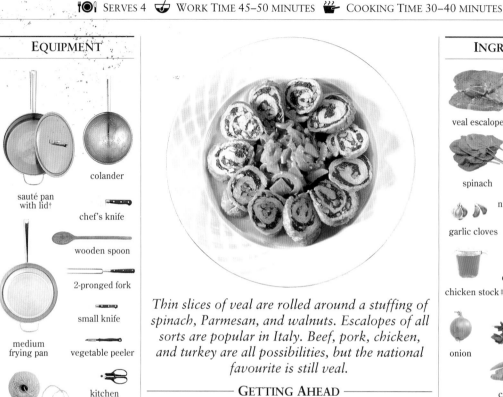

colander

sauté pan with lid†

chef's knife

wooden spoon

2-pronged fork

small knife

medium frying pan

vegetable peeler

kitchen scissors

kitchen string

nutmeg grater

sieve

saucepans

rolling pin

greaseproof paper‡

† shallow casserole can also be used

‡ cling film can also be used

Thin slices of veal are rolled around a stuffing of spinach, Parmesan, and walnuts. Escalopes of all sorts are popular in Italy. Beef, pork, chicken, and turkey are all possibilities, but the national favourite is still veal.

GETTING AHEAD

The veal rolls can be cooked up to 2 days ahead and refrigerated, or they can be frozen. Their flavour mellows on standing. Reheat them, in the sauce, on top of the stove.

metric	SHOPPING LIST	imperial
8	veal escalopes, total weight about 625 g (1¼ lb)	8
1	medium onion	1
1	carrot	1
2	celery sticks	2
30 ml	olive oil, more if needed	2 tbsp
250 ml	dry white wine	8 fl oz
250 ml	chicken stock (see box, page 123), more if needed	8 fl oz
	For the stuffing	
8	garlic cloves	8
45 g	walnuts	1½ oz
500 g	fresh or 300 g (10 oz) defrosted spinach	1 lb
30 ml	olive oil	2 tbsp
30 g	freshly grated Parmesan cheese	1 oz
	salt and pepper	
	freshly grated nutmeg	

INGREDIENTS

veal escalopes

grated Parmesan cheese

spinach

nutmeg†

walnuts

garlic cloves

dry white wine

chicken stock‡

olive oil

onion

celery

carrot

† ground nutmeg can also be used
‡ water can also be used

ANNE SAYS

"Potatoes roasted with olive oil and herbs would make an excellent accompaniment."

ORDER OF WORK

1 PREPARE THE STUFFING; ROLL THE ESCALOPES

2 PREPARE THE VEGETABLES; COOK THE VEAL ROLLS

1 PREPARE THE STUFFING; ROLL THE ESCALOPES

1 Set the flat side of the chef's knife on top of each garlic clove and strike it with your fist. Discard the skins and finely chop the garlic. Coarsely chop the walnuts.

2 If using fresh spinach, wash, cook, and drain the leaves (see box, below). Squeeze defrosted spinach to remove excess water. Using the chef's knife, chop the spinach.

3 Heat the oil in the frying pan and add the spinach. Cook, stirring, until any moisture has evaporated, 2–3 minutes. Remove from the heat and add half of the garlic, the walnuts, Parmesan cheese, salt and pepper, and freshly grated nutmeg. Stir the stuffing ingredients well to combine, and taste for seasoning.

HOW TO PREPARE AND COOK SPINACH

The tough stalks and ribs must be removed from fresh spinach so the leaves will not be stringy after they are cooked. Thorough draining of all moisture after cooking is essential.

1 Tear the tough stalks and ribs from the spinach leaves with your hands. Wash the leaves thoroughly in plenty of cold water.

Stalks are easily pulled off leaves

2 Bring a large saucepan of salted water to boiling, add the spinach and simmer until tender, 1–2 minutes.

3 Drain the spinach in a colander, rinse with cold water, and drain again thoroughly.

4 When cool, squeeze the spinach in your fist to remove excess water.

4 If necessary, flatten the escalopes: put 2 veal slices between 2 sheets of greaseproof paper. Pound to 3 mm (¹⁄₈ inch) thickness with the rolling pin. Repeat with the remaining escalopes.

! TAKE CARE !
Flatten veal gently so holes do not form in the meat.

Pounding veal tenderizes flesh

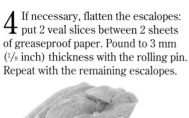

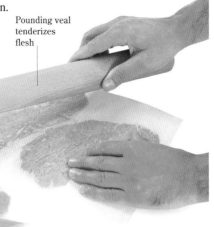

5 Lay 1 veal escalope on the work surface and sprinkle with salt and pepper. Spread about one-eighth of the spinach stuffing on top.

6 Roll up the meat, tucking in the ends. Repeat with the remaining escalopes and spinach stuffing.

7 Tie up the 8 rolls in neat packages. Alternatively, you can secure each roll with a wooden toothpick, threading it in and out along the seam, and catching in the ends.

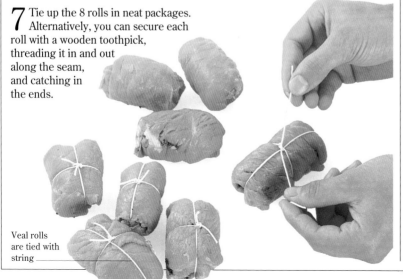

Veal rolls are tied with string

2 PREPARE THE VEGETABLES; COOK THE VEAL ROLLS

1 Peel the onion, leaving a little of the root attached, and cut it lengthwise in half through the root and stalk. Lay each onion half flat on the chopping board and, with the chef's knife, cut it across into thin slices.

Slice all vegetables the same size to cook evenly

2 Peel and trim the carrot. Cut it lengthwise into quarters and then across into thin slices. Thinly slice the celery sticks, with the chef's knife.

3 Heat 30 ml (2 tbsp) olive oil in the sauté pan and add the veal rolls. Cook them over high heat, turning occasionally, until they are well browned on all sides, 2–3 minutes. Transfer the rolls to a plate, using the 2-pronged fork, and set them aside.

4 If necessary, add 1–2 spoonfuls more oil to the sauté pan. Stir in the onion with the remaining garlic and cook, until softened, 2–3 minutes. Add the carrot and celery. Lower the heat and cook, stirring occasionally, until tender, 8–10 minutes. Pour in the wine, bring to a boil, and simmer until reduced by half, 3–5 minutes.

5 Return the veal rolls with any juices to the sauté pan and add the stock with salt and pepper to taste. Cover the pan and simmer, stirring occasionally, until the veal is very tender, 30–40 minutes.

Add more stock during cooking if pan gets dry

Well-browned veal rolls are cooked on bed of vegetables

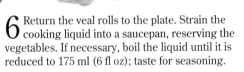

6 Return the veal rolls to the plate. Strain the cooking liquid into a saucepan, reserving the vegetables. If necessary, boil the liquid until it is reduced to 175 ml (6 fl oz); taste for seasoning.

Reserve vegetables for serving with veal rolls

Vegetables cooked with veal rolls are full of flavour

7 Meanwhile, discarding the string or toothpicks, cut the veal rolls across into slices about 1 cm (³/₈ inch) thick. Arrange on warmed individual plates with the vegetables piled in the centre. Spoon on the cooking liquid and serve.

Filling is colourful and crunchy

ROAST LOIN OF PORK WITH GARLIC AND ROSEMARY

Arista

 SERVES 6–8 WORK TIME 15–20 MINUTES ROASTING TIME 1–1½ HOURS

EQUIPMENT

food processor†

medium roasting tin

bowl

rubber spatula

chef's knife   pastry brush

metal skewer

aluminium foil

2-pronged fork

large metal spoon

kitchen string

chopping board

†blender or pestle and mortar can also be used

The Italian name for this boned loin of pork, roasted with a pungent stuffing and coating of garlic, fresh rosemary, and black peppercorns, is taken from the Greek and translates as "the best". What more can I say? Courgette slices sautéed in olive oil with finely chopped shallots make a simple and colourful accompaniment.

GETTING AHEAD

The pork loin can be roasted up to 1 day ahead and refrigerated, tightly wrapped in foil. It is delicious served cold.

metric	SHOPPING LIST	imperial
10	garlic cloves	10
1	small bunch of fresh rosemary	1
10 ml	black peppercorns	2 tsp
	salt	
1.4 kg	boned loin of pork	3 lb
30 ml	olive oil, more for roasting tin	2 tbsp
250 ml	water, more if needed	8 fl oz

INGREDIENTS

boned loin of pork

olive oil   fresh rosemary

garlic cloves   peppercorns

ANNE SAYS
"After the butcher has removed the rib bones from the pork loin, what is left is the eye of meat with a flap of meat attached."

ORDER OF WORK

1 MAKE THE GARLIC AND ROSEMARY STUFFING

2 PREPARE AND STUFF THE LOIN OF PORK

1 MAKE THE GARLIC AND ROSEMARY STUFFING

1 Set the flat side of the chef's knife on top of each garlic clove and strike it with your fist. Discard the skins and put the garlic in the bowl of the food processor.

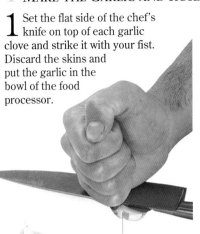

Crushing garlic cloves loosens skin for easy peeling

2 Strip the rosemary leaves from the stalks and add them to the garlic with the peppercorns and salt.

3 Work the ingredients in the food processor, using the pulse button, until finely chopped.

ANNE SAYS
"Keep the mixture coarse if you like pieces of cracked pepper."

2 PREPARE AND STUFF THE LOIN OF PORK

1 Heat the oven to 200°C (400°F, Gas 6). Lightly brush the roasting tin with olive oil.

2 Cut away and discard any excess fat and sinew from the loin of pork, using the chef's knife.

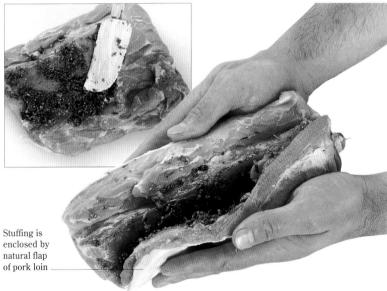

Stuffing is enclosed by natural flap of pork loin

3 Fold open the flap of meat and, using the rubber spatula, spread half of the garlic and rosemary stuffing over the meat. Fold the flap of meat back over the garlic and herb mixture and reshape the loin.

ANNE SAYS
"If your loin of pork does not have a separate flap of meat, make a deep horizontal slit through the meat with the chef's knife, almost to the other side."

4 Using separate pieces of string, tie the pork at 2.5 cm (1 inch) intervals to hold its shape during cooking.

String keeps pork loin in shape during cooking

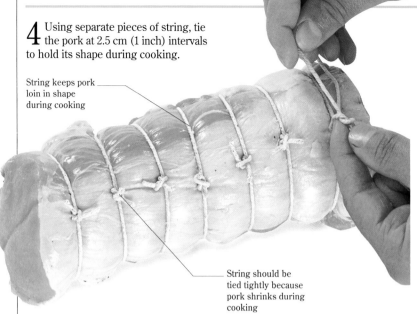

String should be tied tightly because pork shrinks during cooking

5 Set the pork in the prepared roasting tin and spread the remaining stuffing over the outside of the pork. Sprinkle with the olive oil.

6 Roast the pork in the oven until it starts to brown, 20–25 minutes. Remove from the oven and pour half of the water over the pork.

7 Using the 2-pronged fork, turn the meat over. Continue roasting the pork 45–60 minutes longer, turning it 2 or 3 times during cooking so it browns evenly, adding half of the remaining water when the tin becomes dry.

8 The pork is cooked when the skewer inserted in the centre of the loin 30 seconds is very hot to the touch when withdrawn.

9 Transfer the meat to the chopping board, cover it with foil, and let stand for 10 minutes to allow the juices to be reabsorbed before carving.

Foil keeps meat warm while finishing dish

10 Using the large metal spoon, discard some of the fat from the roasting tin. Add the remaining water and boil, stirring, to dissolve the juices in the roasting tin. Taste for seasoning.

11 Discard the strings from the pork and cut the meat into slices about 1 cm (³/₈ inch) thick.

Sharp chef's knife helps in cutting slices of even thickness

Hold loin steady with 2-pronged fork

Lively mixture of garlic, rosemary, and pepper stuffs and tops the meat

🍴 **TO SERVE**
Arrange the pork slices on a warmed serving dish, with courgette slices, if you like; spoon over the cooking juices.

Courgette slices, sautéed in olive oil with chopped shallots, are delicious with pork

V A R I A T I O N

BRAISED PORK WITH MADEIRA SAUCE

In Arrosto di Maiale in Casseruola, *the loin of pork is braised with onions.*

1 Heat the oven to 180°C (350°F, Gas 4). Make the stuffing with 5 garlic cloves, 3–5 sprigs rosemary, and 5 ml (1 tsp) peppercorns. Slice 2 onions.
2 Trim, stuff, and tie up the pork as directed, and season the outside.
3 Heat 45 ml (3 tbsp) olive oil in a casserole. Add the pork, brown on all sides over high heat, about 5 minutes, and remove. Add the onions with 2 bay leaves and cook over medium heat until slightly softened, 3–5 minutes.
4 Return the pork to the pan and pour in 250 ml (8 fl oz) water. Cover and cook in the oven until tender when pierced with a fork, 1³/₄–2 hours. Turn the pork 2–3 times during cooking and add more water if the onions seem dry.
5 Remove the pork and let stand. Mix 15 ml (1 tbsp) Madeira and 5 ml (1 tsp) cornflour to a paste. Spoon off any fat from the cooking liquid. Add 250 ml (8 fl oz) water, bring to a boil, and cook until reduced by half, stirring, 2–3 minutes. Strain into a small pan and heat to boiling. Add 45 ml (3 tbsp) Madeira and bring back to a boil. Whisk in the cornflour mixture until thickened. Taste for seasoning.
6 Slice the pork loin, discarding the strings. Serve with the sauce, and carrot batons, if you like.

HUNTER'S CHICKEN

Pollo alla Cacciatora

🍽 SERVES 4 🥄 WORK TIME 20–25 MINUTES 🍲 COOKING TIME 45–60 MINUTES

EQUIPMENT

slotted spoon

chef's knife

small knife

large sauté pan with lid

wooden spoon

pepper mill

2-pronged fork

large frying pan with lid

chopping board

Alla cacciatora means hunter's style – the Italian way of cooking a bird after a shoot. Add your favourite herb, instead of rosemary, to the sauce – I find that sage works particularly well. The sautéed escarole shown here makes a flavoursome accompaniment.

GETTING AHEAD

The chicken can be cooked up to 2 days ahead and refrigerated in the sauce. Reheat it on top of the stove, adding a little more stock if the sauce seems dry. Prepare the escarole just before serving.

metric	SHOPPING LIST	imperial
1.5 kg	chicken, jointed into 8 pieces	3–3½ lb
	salt and freshly ground black pepper	
60 ml	olive oil	4 tbsp
1	medium onion	1
4	garlic cloves	4
1	sprig of fresh rosemary	1
1	bay leaf	1
60 ml	dry white wine	4 tbsp
125 ml	chicken stock (see box, page 123), more if needed	4 fl oz
1	medium head of escarole, weighing about 750 g (1½ lb)	1
60 ml	water, more if needed	4 tbsp

INGREDIENTS

chicken pieces

olive oil

escarole

fresh rosemary

garlic cloves

chicken stock†

dry white wine

bay leaf

onion

peppercorns

†water can also be used

ANNE SAYS

"Two heads of radicchio, total weight 375–425 g (12–14 oz), can be substituted for the escarole. Prepare them in the same way, cutting each head into 4 pieces."

ORDER OF WORK

1 SAUTE THE CHICKEN

2 SAUTE THE ESCAROLE

1 SAUTE THE CHICKEN

1 Season the chicken pieces all over with salt and freshly ground black pepper to taste.

Chicken is sprinkled with black pepper

2 Heat half of the oil in the sauté pan over medium heat. Add the chicken thighs and drumsticks, skin-side down, and sauté until they begin to brown, about 5 minutes.

3 Add the chicken breast pieces, and continue cooking gently until very brown, 10–15 minutes. Turn and brown the other side.

4 Meanwhile, peel the onion, leaving a little of the root attached, and cut lengthwise in half.

5 Slice each onion half horizontally towards the root, leaving the slices attached at the root end, then slice vertically, again leaving the root end uncut. Finally, cut across the onion to make dice.

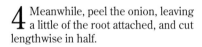

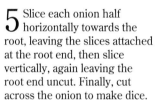

6 Set the flat side of the chef's knife on top of each garlic clove and strike it with your fist. Discard the skins and finely chop the garlic.

Skin of chicken is browned and crispy

Move chicken pieces to side of pan to make space in centre

7 Add the chopped onion and half of the chopped garlic to the chicken, letting them fall to the bottom of the pan. Continue cooking gently until they are soft and golden brown, about 10 minutes.

At end of cooking, sauce is dark and reduced

9 Cover and simmer until the chicken is tender when pierced with the 2-pronged fork, 15–20 minutes. If the pan becomes dry during cooking, add a little more chicken stock. If some pieces of chicken cook before others, remove them from the pan and keep them warm. While the chicken is cooking, sauté the escarole.

8 Add the sprig of rosemary, bay leaf, wine, chicken stock, salt, and pepper, and stir to mix.

2 SAUTE THE ESCAROLE

1 With the small knife, trim off the root end of the escarole. Discard any tough, green outer leaves, then wash well.

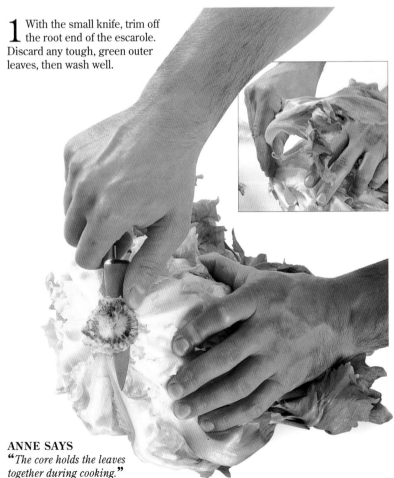

2 Using the chef's knife, cut the escarole into 8 wedges, cutting through the core.

3 Heat the remaining oil in the frying pan. Add the rest of the garlic with the escarole, water, salt, and pepper. Bring to a boil, then cover and simmer gently, 10–20 minutes, depending on the toughness of the vegetable. Turn the escarole occasionally.

ANNE SAYS
"The core holds the leaves together during cooking."

4 Test that the escarole is tender by piercing near the core with a knife. The liquid should have evaporated so the leaves are lightly glazed with oil.

ANNE SAYS
"If the escarole produces a great deal of liquid, remove the lid for the last 5–10 minutes of cooking so it can evaporate."

Sauce is thickened and reduced when chicken is cooked

5 Remove the chicken pieces from the pan and arrange on warmed individual plates. Discard the bay leaf and rosemary from the sauce, and taste for seasoning.

¶©¶ TO SERVE
Arrange the escarole next to the chicken, tucking large leaves under small ones to make neat packages. Spoon the sauce over the chicken and serve with crusty bread.

Chicken is meltingly tender and full of flavour

Sautéed escarole is lightly glazed with olive oil and flavoured with garlic

V A R I A T I O N

HUNTER'S CHICKEN WITH BLACK OLIVES

Pollo alla Cacciatora con le Olive is a real treat for olive lovers. It is served here with sautéed chicory.

1 Omit the onion, chicken stock, rosemary, and bay leaf from the main recipe. Chop 5 garlic cloves.
2 Stone 195 g (6 ½ oz) oil-cured black olives. Chop half of the olives, leaving the rest whole. Chop 2 anchovy fillets.
3 Heat half of the oil in a large sauté pan and add half of the chopped garlic. Add the seasoned chicken pieces as directed, and sauté until all pieces are browned, 10–15 minutes.
4 Add the wine, 30 ml (2 tbsp) red wine vinegar, the chopped and whole olives, and the anchovies to the chicken. Cover and simmer the chicken as directed, adding a little water if the pan becomes dry.
5 Meanwhile, trim 2 medium heads of chicory, total weight about 250 g (8 oz). Wipe them with a damp paper towel and discard any wilted leaves. Cut each head lengthwise into quarters, cutting through the core.
6 Cook the chicory as for the escarole, until lightly browned.
7 Serve the chicken and chicory on warmed plates. Spoon the olive sauce over the chicken.

STRAWBERRY AND RASPBERRY HAZELNUT TART

Crostata di Fragole e Lamponi

🍽 SERVES 6–8   🥣 WORK TIME 35–40 MINUTES*   🍲 BAKING TIME 30–35 MINUTES

EQUIPMENT

food processor †

23–25 cm (9–10 inch) flan tin, with removable base

bowls

piping bag and medium star nozzle

small knife

pastry brush

baking sheet

chef's knife

sieve

whisk ‡

rubber spatula

palette knife

wooden spoon

chopping board

pastry scraper

† blender can also be used
‡ electric mixer can also be used

INGREDIENTS

strawberries

icing sugar

granulated sugar

hazelnuts

raspberries

plain flour

unsalted butter

double cream

Marsala wine   egg

Traditionally, Italian fruit tarts are simple – often nothing more than fresh fruit on a pastry base. Here, red berries top hazelnut pastry, decked with Marsala-accented whipped cream.

GETTING AHEAD

The dough can be made up to 2 days ahead and refrigerated, or it can be frozen. You can bake the hazelnut pastry round 6–8 hours ahead. Assemble the tart not more than 2 hours before serving.

*plus 45 minutes chilling time

metric	SHOPPING LIST	imperial
250 ml	double cream	8 fl oz
45–60 ml	icing sugar	3–4 tbsp
30 ml	Marsala wine	2 tbsp
300 g	strawberries	10 oz
125 g	raspberries	4 oz
	For the hazelnut pastry dough	
125 g	hazelnuts	4 oz
75 g	granulated sugar	2 ½ oz
125 g	plain flour, more if needed	4 oz
125 g	unsalted butter, more for flan tin	4 oz
1	egg	1

ORDER OF WORK

1. MAKE THE HAZELNUT PASTRY DOUGH

2. BAKE THE HAZELNUT PASTRY

3. ASSEMBLE THE TART

MAKE THE HAZELNUT PASTRY DOUGH

1 Toast and skin the hazelnuts (see box, right). Reserve 8 hazelnuts for garnish. In the food processor, grind the remaining hazelnuts, with the sugar, to a fine powder. Alternatively, grind them with the sugar in 2–3 batches in a blender.

! TAKE CARE !
Do not overwork or the oil from the nuts will create a paste.

HOW TO TOAST AND SKIN NUTS

Toasting nuts intensifies their flavour and adds crunch to their texture. It also loosens the skins from nuts such as hazelnuts for easy removal.

Hazelnut skins will come off easily after toasting

1 Heat the oven to 180°C (350°F, Gas 4). Toast the nuts on a baking sheet until lightly browned, stirring occasionally, 12–15 minutes.

2 While the nuts are still hot, rub them in a rough tea towel to remove their skins, then let cool.

2 Sift the flour onto a work surface, add the ground nut mixture, and make a large well in the centre.

3 Cut the butter into pieces and add the pieces to the well in the centre of the flour.

4 Add the egg and, using your fingertips, work the ingredients in the well until soft and thoroughly mixed.

Butter, egg, and sugar are blended with fingertips

5 Draw the hazelnut powder and the flour into the centre, using the pastry scraper. Work them into the butter mixture with your fingers to form coarse crumbs.

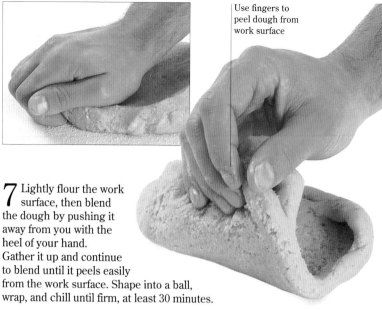

Use fingers to peel dough from work surface

6 Continue working so the crumbs start sticking together. Press the crumbs together with your fingertips to form a ball of dough.

7 Lightly flour the work surface, then blend the dough by pushing it away from you with the heel of your hand. Gather it up and continue to blend until it peels easily from the work surface. Shape into a ball, wrap, and chill until firm, at least 30 minutes.

2 BAKE THE HAZELNUT PASTRY

1 Heat the oven to 180°C (350°F, Gas 4). Brush the flan tin with melted butter, using the pastry brush.

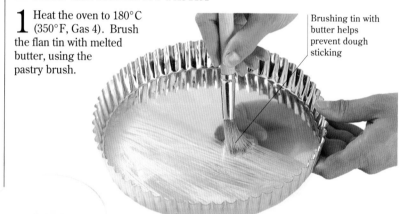

Brushing tin with butter helps prevent dough sticking

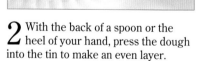

2 With the back of a spoon or the heel of your hand, press the dough into the tin to make an even layer.

3 Chill the dough until firm, at least 15 minutes. Bake in the heated oven until the pastry is golden brown and shrinking slightly from the side of the tin, 30–35 minutes.

ANNE SAYS
"Baking the pastry until golden gives the hazelnuts a full toasted flavour."

4 Set the flan tin on the top of a bowl so the side will loosen. Transfer the pastry round on the base of the tin to a serving plate. Let cool.

3 ASSEMBLE THE TART

Flavourings are added when cream is still soft

1 Make the Marsala whipped cream: using the whisk, whip the double cream in a chilled bowl until it forms soft peaks.

2 Add the icing sugar and Marsala. Continue whipping until the cream forms stiff peaks.

Chilled bowl helps give volume to whipped cream

3 Pick over the raspberries. Hull the strawberries, and wash them only if they are dirty.

Moist green hull indicates freshness

Tip of knife scoops hull from strawberry

4 With the small knife, cut the strawberries in half, or into quarters if they are large.

5 Using the palette knife, spread two-thirds of the Marsala whipped cream evenly over the cooled hazelnut pastry, just to the edge.

! TAKE CARE !
Washing softens strawberries, so only wash them if absolutely necessary.

Pastry bag is twisted over thumb to control flow of Marsala cream

6 Starting at the outer edge and working inwards, arrange the strawberries in concentric circles on the Marsala whipped cream. Arrange the raspberries in a pile in the centre of the cream, leaving about 1.25 cm (1/2 inch) space between the strawberries and raspberries for piping rosettes.

7 Put the rest of the Marsala cream into the piping bag fitted with the star nozzle. Pipe a ring of cream rosettes between the strawberries and raspberries, and 8 large rosettes around the outside edge, on the strawberries. Place 1 reserved hazelnut in the centre of each rosette. Chill until serving.

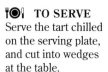 **TO SERVE**
Serve the tart chilled on the serving plate, and cut into wedges at the table.

Toasted hazelnut pastry makes a crunchy base for berry and cream tart

Marsala wine in rosettes of whipped cream gives an Italian touch to fruit tart

Hazelnut garnish indicates flavouring in pastry

VARIATION

STRAWBERRY TART WITH CHOCOLATE CREAM

Here, in Crostata di Fragole al Cioccolato, *a layer of rich chocolate cream is spread on an almond pastry base to make a perfect background for a topping of fresh strawberries. Raspberries can be substituted for the strawberries, if you like.*

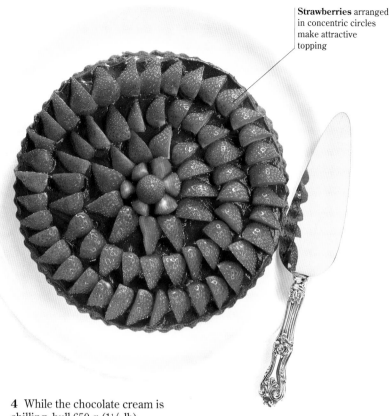

Strawberries arranged in concentric circles make attractive topping

1 Make the pastry dough as directed in the main recipe, substituting 125 g (4 oz) whole blanched almonds for the hazelnuts. Bake as directed.

2 Chop 125 g (4 oz) plain chocolate into small chunks.

3 Omit the Marsala whipped cream. Put 125 ml (4 fl oz) double cream and the chopped chocolate in a medium saucepan and heat, stirring occasionally with a wooden spoon, until the chocolate is melted and smooth, 3–5 minutes. Let cool slightly, then refrigerate just until cold, stirring occasionally.

4 While the chocolate cream is chilling, hull 650 g (1¹/₃ lb) strawberries, washing them only if dirty, and cut them in half, or in quarters if large. Omit the raspberries.

5 Using an electric beater or a whisk, beat the chilled chocolate cream until fluffy and light in colour, 3–5 minutes. Do not overbeat the mixture or it may separate, becoming grainy.

6 With a palette knife, spread the chocolate cream over the cooled almond pastry to form a smooth, even layer.

7 Arrange the strawberries, cut-side down, in concentric circles, on top of the chocolate cream.

8 Cut the tart into wedges and serve on individual plates.

Crisp almond base contrasts with smooth chocolate

RICOTTA CHEESECAKE

Crostata di Ricotta

 SERVES 8–10 WORK TIME 35–40 MINUTES* BAKING TIME 1–1¼ HOURS

EQUIPMENT

23–25 cm (9–10 inch) springform tin

 sieve

 chef's knife

bowls

 pastry brush

small knife

 wooden spoon

grater

rolling pin

greaseproof paper   pastry scraper

baking sheet

chopping board

ANNE SAYS
"A springform cake tin is necessary because the cheesecake cannot be inverted for removal from the tin after baking."

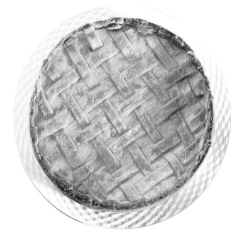

When I first tasted a classic Italian cheesecake of fresh ricotta flavoured with candied orange peel and almonds, baked in a sweet lemon pastry crust, I knew that this was perfection. The fresher the cheese, the better the cake.

GETTING AHEAD

The cheesecake can be made up to 1 day ahead and kept refrigerated. The flavour will mellow, but the texture will not be as light.

*plus 45–60 minutes chilling time

metric	SHOPPING LIST	imperial
1	orange	1
30 ml	chopped candied orange peel	2 tbsp
1.25 kg	ricotta cheese	2½ lb
100 g	caster sugar	3¼ oz
15 ml	plain flour	1 tbsp
	salt	
5 ml	vanilla essence	1 tsp
45 g	sultanas	1½ oz
30 g	slivered almonds	1 oz
4	egg yolks	4
	For the sweet pastry dough	
175 g	unsalted butter, more for cake tin	6 oz
250 g	plain flour, more if needed	8 oz
1	lemon	1
50 g	caster sugar	1¾ oz
4	egg yolks	4
1	whole egg, for glaze	1

INGREDIENTS

orange

ricotta cheese

vanilla essence

unsalted butter

lemon

sultanas

plain flour

egg yolks

candied orange peel

slivered almonds

whole egg

caster sugar

ORDER OF WORK

1 MAKE THE SWEET PASTRY DOUGH

2 ROLL OUT DOUGH AND LINE THE TIN

3 MAKE THE FILLING

4 MAKE THE LATTICE AND BAKE THE CHEESECAKE

1 MAKE THE SWEET PASTRY DOUGH

ANNE SAYS
"It is important that the well in the flour is made large enough so that the ingredients can be mixed together easily."

Softened butter will blend easily with sugar

Egg yolks enrich dough and help give golden colour to finished pastry

1 Using the rolling pin, pound the butter between 2 sheets of greaseproof paper to soften it slightly.

2 Sift the flour onto a work surface and make a large well in the centre. Grate the zest from the lemon.

3 Put the sugar, butter, egg yolks, a pinch of salt, and the grated lemon zest in the centre of the well.

Work butter with egg yolk and sugar

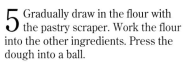

4 Using your fingertips, work together all the ingredients in the well until they are thoroughly mixed.

5 Gradually draw in the flour with the pastry scraper. Work the flour into the other ingredients. Press the dough into a ball.

6 Lightly flour the work surface, then blend the dough by pushing it away from you with the heel of your hand. Gather the dough up with the pastry scraper and continue to blend until the dough is very smooth and peels away from the work surface in one piece, 1–2 minutes.

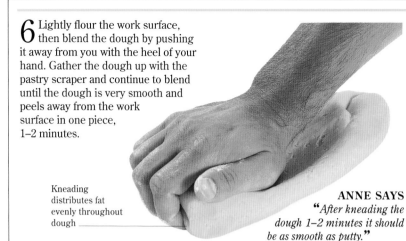

Kneading distributes fat evenly throughout dough

ANNE SAYS
"After kneading the dough 1–2 minutes it should be as smooth as putty."

7 Shape the dough into a ball, wrap it, and chill it in the refrigerator until firm, about 30 minutes.

2 ROLL OUT DOUGH AND LINE THE TIN

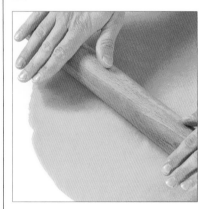

1 Brush the bottom and side of the springform tin with melted butter. Lightly flour the work surface and roll out three-quarters of the dough to make a 35–37 cm (14–15 inch) round.

2 Roll up the dough around the rolling pin, then unroll it loosely so that it drapes over the prepared tin.

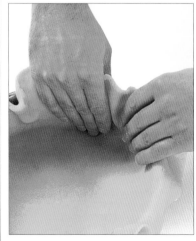

3 Lift the edge of the dough with one hand and press it well into the bottom of the tin with the other hand. Press the dough gently up the side of the tin with your fingers.

4 Using a table knife, trim excess dough even with the outer edge of the tin. Chill the shell, together with the remaining dough and trimmings, 15 minutes. Meanwhile, make the filling.

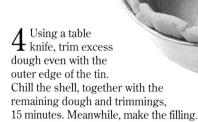

Excess dough will be trimmed level with tin edge

3 MAKE THE FILLING

1 Grate the zest from the orange onto a small plate. Finely chop the candied orange peel.

2 Place the ricotta in a large bowl and beat in the sugar, flour, and 2.5 ml (½ tsp) salt.

3 Add the grated orange zest, candied peel, vanilla essence, sultanas, slivered almonds, and egg yolks to the ricotta. Beat the mixture together thoroughly to combine.

Egg yolks will bind cheese mixture so it sets during baking

Slivered almonds give crunch to filling

4 Spoon the filling into the chilled pastry shell. Tap the tin on the work surface to eliminate any air pockets. Smooth the top of the filling, using the back of the wooden spoon.

4 MAKE THE LATTICE AND BAKE THE CHEESECAKE

1 Press any dough trimmings into the remaining dough and roll it into a 25 cm (10 inch) round on a lightly floured surface. Using the chef's knife, cut the dough into strips about 1.25 cm (½ inch) wide.

Alternate strips are folded back

2 Lay half the strips, left to right, across the filling, 2 cm (¾ inch) apart, so any ends hang over the edge of the tin. Fold back alternate strips halfway. Set a new strip across the strips in the centre of the filling.

3 Unfold the folded strips to cover the crosswise strip, again leaving ends to hang over the edge of the tin.

Ends are left to hang over edge of tin

4 Fold back the alternate strips. Place the next strip about 2 cm (³/₄ inch) from the first.

Lay strips loosely over filling so they do not shrink during baking

Weave dough strips in symmetrical pattern

Dough strips should be even

5 Cover the second crosswise strip by unfolding the folded strips across it. Continue to fold back alternate strips as before.

6 Repeat with a third crosswise strip. By this stage, half of the surface should be latticed.

7 Turn the pan 180° and repeat the process on the other half of the cheesecake, in the same way, so the whole cake is latticed.

Interwoven lattice looks appealing on top of cheesecake

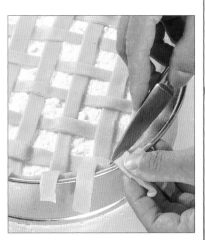

8 With the small knife, carefully trim off the overhanging ends of dough, so that the pastry strips are even with the edge of the pastry shell.

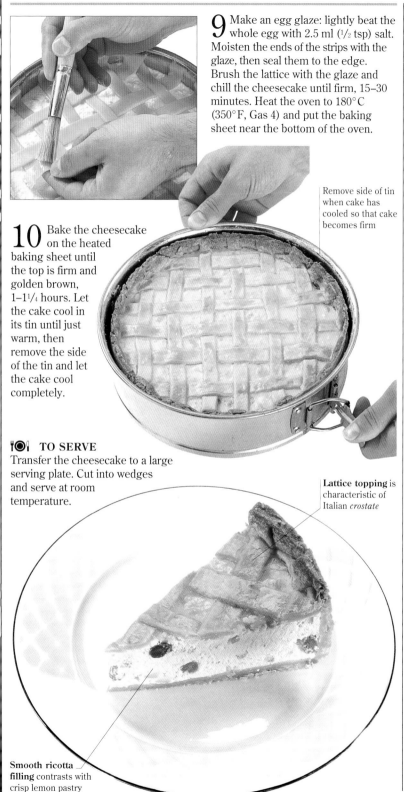

9 Make an egg glaze: lightly beat the whole egg with 2.5 ml (¹/₂ tsp) salt. Moisten the ends of the strips with the glaze, then seal them to the edge. Brush the lattice with the glaze and chill the cheesecake until firm, 15–30 minutes. Heat the oven to 180°C (350°F, Gas 4) and put the baking sheet near the bottom of the oven.

Remove side of tin when cake has cooled so that cake becomes firm

10 Bake the cheesecake on the heated baking sheet until the top is firm and golden brown, 1–1¹/₄ hours. Let the cake cool in its tin until just warm, then remove the side of the tin and let the cake cool completely.

|O| TO SERVE
Transfer the cheesecake to a large serving plate. Cut into wedges and serve at room temperature.

Lattice topping is characteristic of Italian *crostate*

Smooth ricotta filling contrasts with crisp lemon pastry

CHOCOLATE RICOTTA PIE

I discovered this delicious Crostata di Ricotta al Cioccolato *in a pastry shop in Assisi.*

1 Make the sweet pastry dough as directed in the main recipe, with 175 g (6 oz) flour, 3 egg yolks, 45 g (1¹/₂ oz) sugar, and 125 g (4 oz) butter; omit the lemon zest.
2 Roll out all the pastry dough to line a 33 x 23 x 5 cm (13 x 9 x 2 inch) buttered baking dish. The pastry dough crust should be about 3 cm (1¹/₄ inches) high around the sides.
3 Using a chef's knife, finely chop 125 g (4 oz) plain chocolate; or chop it in a food processor.
4 Make the filling as directed, adding the chopped chocolate and grated orange zest in place of the candied fruit, sultanas, and almonds.
5 Fill the prepared pastry dough shell, chill, and bake as directed until set, 35–40 minutes. Let the pie cool completely, in the baking dish.
6 Chop 30 g (1 oz) more chocolate. Melt it in a bowl in a saucepan of hot water, stirring until it is smooth. Stir in 2.5 ml (¹/₂ tsp) vegetable oil.
7 Dip the tines of a fork in the melted chocolate and flick over the top of the pie so that the chocolate makes a freeform lattice.
8 Cut the pie into bars and serve on individual plates.

WALNUT CAKE WITH CARAMEL TOPPING

Torta di Noci

🍽 SERVES 8 🥄 WORK TIME 25–30 MINUTES ♨ BAKING TIME 1–1¼ HOURS

EQUIPMENT

food processor

bowls

wire rack

medium saucepan

greaseproof paper

kitchen scissors

whisk

pastry brush

palette knife

grater

pencil

rubber spatula

metal skewer

wooden spoon

23 cm (9 inch) round cake tin

A crisp layer of caramel tops this rich walnut cake flavoured with grappa or rum – fare for a celebration, but surprisingly simple to make.

GETTING AHEAD

The cake can be stored up to 2 days in an airtight container; the flavour will mellow. Add the caramel topping just before serving because it softens on standing.

INGREDIENTS

lemon

white bread

eggs

walnuts

unsalted butter

grappa†

caster sugar

†rum can also be used

ANNE SAYS

"Grappa is the Italian equivalent of marc, a spirit made by distilling the remains of white grapes that have been crushed to make wine. It may be flavoured with herbs."

metric	SHOPPING LIST	imperial
1	lemon	1
2	slices of white bread	2
175 g	walnut halves	6 oz
4	eggs	4
125 g	unsalted butter, more for cake tin	4 oz
135 g	caster sugar	4½ oz
30 ml	grappa	2 tbsp
	For the topping	
60 ml	water	4 tbsp
100 g	sugar	3¼ oz

ORDER OF WORK

1 PREPARE AND BAKE THE CAKE

2 MAKE THE TOPPING AND COAT THE CAKE

PREPARE AND BAKE THE CAKE

Cake tin should be correct size to ensure successful results

Cut around pencil line so paper will fit base of tin exactly

1 Heat the oven to 180°C (350°F, Gas 4). Using the base of the cake tin, draw a circle on the greaseproof paper and cut it out.

2 Brush the bottom and side of the cake tin with melted butter and line the bottom with the greaseproof paper round. Brush the paper with more melted butter.

Walnuts and crumbs give cake its characteristic texture

Dryness of bread helps prevent nuts becoming oily when they are ground

3 Grate the zest from the lemon. Toast the bread in the heated oven until very dry, 5–7 minutes; do not let it brown. Break the bread into pieces and put them in the food processor. Work until finely ground, using the pulse button. Alternatively, grind the bread in a rotary cheese grater.

4 Reserve 8 walnut halves for garnish. Add the remaining walnuts to the food processor and grind until quite fine. Alternatively, finely chop the nuts with a chef's knife.

! TAKE CARE !
Do not overwork the nuts in the processor or they will form a paste. You may like to leave a few chunks for texture.

5 Separate the eggs (see page 105). Cream the butter, using the wooden spoon or an electric mixer. Add two-thirds of the sugar and beat until light and fluffy, 2–3 minutes.

Wooden spoon or electric mixer can be used for creaming

Butter is creamed before sugar is added so that sugar will be easy to incorporate

6 Add the egg yolks, one at a time, to the creamed butter and sugar, beating well after each addition.

7 Add the grated lemon zest and grappa, and beat into the batter.

ANNE SAYS
"Beat the batter well to develop the flavour in the lemon zest."

8 Add the ground walnuts and breadcrumbs to the batter and stir well to combine.

9 Whisk the egg whites until stiff (see box, page 106). Sprinkle with the remaining sugar and whisk until glossy, about 20 seconds longer. Gently fold one-quarter of the egg whites into the batter.

Cut and fold meringue into batter

Add heavier mixture to lighter one when folding

10 Add the egg white and walnut mixture to the remaining egg whites. Cut down into the centre of the bowl, scoop under the contents, and turn them over in a rolling motion. At the same time, turn the bowl anti-clockwise.

11 Spoon the batter into the prepared cake tin and smooth the top with the rubber spatula. Bake in the heated oven until the metal skewer inserted in the centre of the cake comes out clean, 1–1¼ hours.

Buttered paper is easy to peel from cake

12 Let the cake cool slightly, then invert it onto the wire rack. Peel off and discard the paper, and let the cake cool completely.

Wire rack lets air circulate

HOW TO SEPARATE EGGS

Eggs are easy to separate if you use the shell. However, if an egg shell is contaminated with salmonella, bacteria can cling to the shell and spread. Alternative methods are filtering the white through your fingers or using an egg separator.

1 To separate an egg with the shell: crack the egg at its broadest point by tapping it against a bowl. With 2 thumbs, break it open, letting some white slip over the edge of the shell into the bowl.

2 Tip the yolk from one half of the shell to the other, detaching the remaining white from the yolk. If yolk slips into the white, remove it with the shell. To remove white threads, pinch them against the side of the shell with your fingers.

To separate an egg with your fingers: crack the egg into a bowl. Hold your cupped fingers over another bowl and let the white fall through them, leaving the yolk.

HOW TO WHISK EGG WHITES UNTIL STIFF

Egg whites should be whisked until stiff but not dry. In order for them to whisk properly, the bowl and whisk must be completely free from any trace of water, grease, or egg yolk. A copper bowl and a large balloon whisk are the classic French utensils for whisking egg whites. A metal or glass bowl with a balloon whisk or an electric mixer can also be used.

1 Begin whisking whites slowly. When they become foamy and white, increase the whisking speed. If you like, add a small pinch of salt or cream of tartar to help achieve maximum volume.

! TAKE CARE !
Do not slow down the whisking once the whites form soft peaks or they may "turn", becoming grainy.

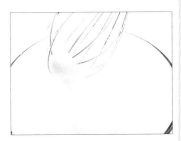

2 The whites are whisked enough if they form a stiff peak when the whisk is lifted, gathering in the whisk wires and sticking without falling. The whites should be used at once because they quickly separate on standing.

! TAKE CARE !
Do not overbeat the egg whites; if they are overbeaten, the correct texture cannot be reconstituted.

2 MAKE THE TOPPING AND COAT THE CAKE

1 Heat the water and sugar in the saucepan over low heat until the sugar has dissolved. Boil, without stirring, until the syrup starts to turn golden.

Bubbles start to break more slowly and turn golden around edge of pan

Boil sugar syrup briskly so water evaporates rapidly

! TAKE CARE !
If the sugar syrup is stirred during boiling it may crystallize.

2 Lower the heat and continue cooking, swirling the syrup in the pan once or twice so it colours evenly.

3 Cook until the caramel is deep golden in colour for best flavour. Do not overcook or caramel may burn.

Protect hand with tea towel from hot handle and rising steam

Cold water will quickly cool base of pan

4 Quickly plunge the base of the pan into a bowl of cold water to stop the caramel cooking.

Hold palette knife at an angle when spreading caramel

Spread caramel quickly because it sets as soon as it is cool

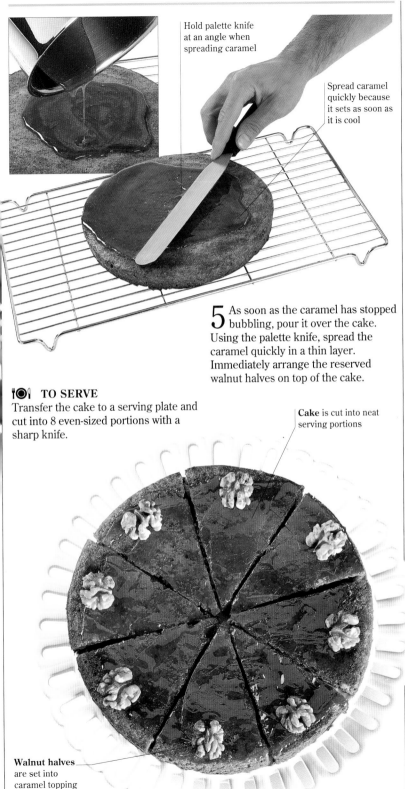

5 As soon as the caramel has stopped bubbling, pour it over the cake. Using the palette knife, spread the caramel quickly in a thin layer. Immediately arrange the reserved walnut halves on top of the cake.

🍽 TO SERVE

Transfer the cake to a serving plate and cut into 8 even-sized portions with a sharp knife.

Cake is cut into neat serving portions

Walnut halves are set into caramel topping

V A R I A T I O N

WALNUT CAKE WITH RAISINS

Torta di Noci e Uve Passe packs an added punch: the raisins are soaked in grappa.

1 Put 150 g (5 oz) raisins in a small, shallow bowl. Add 125 ml (4 fl oz) grappa and let stand 15 minutes.
2 Drain the raisins and reserve the grappa. Make the cake as directed in the main recipe, using all the walnuts for the batter and adding the raisins with the lemon zest. Bake as directed.
3 While the cake is still warm, spoon on the reserved grappa.
4 Omit the caramel topping. Cut 4 or 5 strips of light cardboard about 2 cm (³/₄ inch) wide and lay them on top of the cake. Sift icing sugar evenly over the cake. Carefully lift off the strips and discard the excess sugar.
5 Lay the strips back on the cake to make a diagonal lattice and cover again with sifted icing sugar; you will need about 60 g (2 oz) in total. Again, carefully lift off the cardboard strips.
6 Transfer the cake to a serving plate and serve.

GRAPEFRUIT GRANITA

Granita di Pompelmo

🍽 SERVES 4 ⌣ WORK TIME 15–20 MINUTES ❄ FREEZING TIME 5–6 HOURS*

EQUIPMENT

chef's knife

whisk

small saucepan

vegetable peeler

lemon squeezer

small sieve

non-metallic bowl

greaseproof paper

chopping board

ANNE SAYS
"*In this recipe, a whisk is used to break up the ice, but you can also make granita using a food processor or blender: pour the grapefruit mixture into ice cube trays and freeze until set, 2–3 hours. When frozen, transfer the ice cubes to a food processor or blender and work until slushy.*"

Grapefruit granita, served here with All Souls' Day almond biscuits, is a refreshing end to a rich dinner. Sweetened grapefruit and lemon juices are put directly in the freezer and frozen into a granita. Unlike a smooth sorbet, the texture of a granita should resemble coarse snow – instead of using a churn, this effect is achieved by whisking the fruit juice and sugar mixture at hourly intervals, to break up the ice crystals as they form.

GETTING AHEAD
The granita can be made up to 2 days ahead and kept in the freezer. If the ice mixture has solidified, leave it at room temperature until slushy. Whisk it and refreeze 30–60 minutes, or grind it in a food processor just before serving.

* *stir mixture about once an hour*

INGREDIENTS

grapefruit

lemon

sugar

almond biscuits (optional)

ANNE SAYS
"*Pink grapefruit will give the granita a pretty colour, but as these grapefruit are sweeter than white grapefruit, you may need to reduce the sugar slightly.*"

ORDER OF WORK

1 MAKE AND FREEZE THE GRAPEFRUIT GRANITA

2 MAKE THE CANDIED GRAPEFRUIT ZEST AND SERVE THE GRANITA

metric	SHOPPING LIST	imperial
3	medium grapefruit	3
1/2	lemon	1/2
50 g	sugar, more to taste	1 3/4 oz
30 ml	water	2 tbsp
	All Souls' Day almond biscuits (see box, page 110) for serving (optional)	

1 MAKE AND FREEZE THE GRAPEFRUIT GRANITA

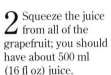

Pale yellow grapefruit juice makes delicate-coloured granita

1 Thinly pare the zest from half of 1 grapefruit, leaving behind the white pith. Reserve the pared zest.

2 Squeeze the juice from all of the grapefruit; you should have about 500 ml (16 fl oz) juice.

ANNE SAYS
"To extract maximum juice, roll the grapefruit firmly on the work surface with the palm of your hand."

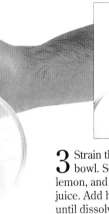

3 Strain the juice into the non-metallic bowl. Squeeze the juice from the lemon, and strain into the grapefruit juice. Add half of the sugar and stir until dissolved. Taste, adding more sugar if you like.

4 Freeze the liquid until ice starts to form on top, 45–60 minutes. Whisk to break the ice.

Strain grapefruit and lemon juices to remove any pips and small pieces of pulp

5 Continue freezing, whisking the mixture to break the ice about once an hour, until the granita is slushy and slightly granular. Allow 4–5 hours.

MAKE THE CANDIED GRAPEFRUIT ZEST AND SERVE THE GRANITA

1 With the chef's knife, cut the pared grapefruit zest into very fine julienne strips.

2 In the small saucepan, heat the remaining 30 ml (2 tbsp) sugar with the water until the sugar has dissolved. Add the grapefruit zest.

ALL SOULS' DAY ALMOND BISCUITS

Chewy and moist, these almond biscuits – Fave dei Morti – are a tradition on All Souls' Day in Italy. They are delicious with granita and other iced desserts, or just as a snack with coffee. The biscuits can be stored up to 1 week in an airtight container.

🍽 MAKES 24–30

🥣 WORK TIME 15–20 MINUTES

🍲 BAKING TIME 15–20 MINUTES

metric	SHOPPING LIST	imperial
1	lemon	1
90 g	plain flour	3 oz
1	egg	1
155 g	ground almonds	5 oz
125 g	caster sugar	4 oz
15 ml	brandy	1 tbsp
15 g	butter	1/2 oz
12–15	whole, blanched almonds	12–15

1 Heat the oven to 180°C (350°F, Gas 4). Butter a baking sheet. Sprinkle it with flour and discard the excess. Grate the zest from the lemon. Sift the flour, and whisk the egg.

2 Mix together the ground almonds, sugar, brandy, flour, butter, and lemon zest. Add the egg; stir until the dough holds together and does not stick to the bowl.

3 Wet your hands and roll the dough into 2.5 cm (1 inch) balls. Place on the prepared baking sheet, leaving 2.5 cm (1 inch) between the biscuits.

Gaps are left between biscuits to allow for spreading during baking

4 Split the almonds in half, and press a half into the top of each biscuit. Bake towards the top of the heated oven until lightly browned, 15–20 minutes. Remove from the oven; let cool 5 minutes before transferring to a wire rack to cool completely.

3 Simmer the zest until all the water has evaporated and the zest is translucent and tender, 12–15 minutes.

4 Spread the grapefruit zest on a sheet of greaseproof paper with a fork, and let it cool.

5 Spoon the grapefruit granita into 4 chilled coupe glasses. Pile the candied zest on top and serve at once. If you like, All Souls' Day almond biscuits can be served on the side.

Coupe glasses must be well chilled or granita may melt

Use chilled spoon, and work as fast as possible because granita melts quickly

Glass coupe dish displays icy granita at its best

All Souls' Day biscuits are an Italian speciality resembling macaroons

VARIATION
COFFEE GRANITA

A favourite in Italian cafés, Granita di Caffè is made from sweetened espresso, topped here with Amaretto-flavoured whipped cream. This recipe serves 6 people.

1 Bring 1 litre (1²/₃ pints) water to a boil. Whisk 90 g (3 oz) ground espresso or dark-roast coffee into the water, cover, and let stand 10 minutes.
2 Pour the mixture through a sieve, then through a coffee filter, and measure 750 ml (1¼ pints) liquid.
3 Stir 100 g (3½ oz) granulated sugar into the coffee until dissolved. Taste, adding more sugar if you like, and let the mixture cool to room temperature. Freeze as directed in the main recipe.
4 Put 6 stemmed glasses in the refrigerator to chill.
5 Using a whisk or electric mixer, whip 125 ml (4 fl oz) double cream in a chilled bowl until it forms soft peaks.
6 Add 15 ml (1 tbsp) icing sugar and 15–30 ml (1–2 tbsp) Amaretto liqueur, and continue whipping until the cream forms stiff peaks.
7 Fill a piping bag fitted with a medium star nozzle with the whipped cream.
8 Spoon the coffee granita into the chilled stemmed glasses. Pipe a large rosette of whipped cream on the top of each. If you like, top each rosette with chocolate-covered espresso beans.

APPLE CAKE

Torta di Mele

🍽 SERVES 8 　 WORK TIME 20–25 MINUTES 　 BAKING TIME 1¼–1½ HOURS

EQUIPMENT

bowls

23–25 cm
(9–10 inch)
springform tin

melon baller†

thin-bladed knife

pastry brush

small saucepan

vegetable peeler

small knife

electric mixer‡

grater

sieve

rubber spatula

metal skewer

chopping board

†teaspoon can also be used
‡wooden spoon can also be used

INGREDIENTS

apples

unsalted butter

plain flour

milk

eggs

sugar

baking
powder

lemon

ANNE SAYS
"*Most lemons we buy are coated with wax to prevent loss of moisture, so wash them before grating.*"

A firm dessert apple is best for this moist and dense cake, which is perfect for picnics. Any flavourful apple that holds its shape during cooking, such as a Granny Smith, is appropriate. Italian cooks often use Golden Delicious apples, now grown worldwide.

— GETTING AHEAD —

The cake is best eaten warm from the oven, but it can be stored up to 2 days in an airtight container.

metric	SHOPPING LIST	imperial
175 g	plain flour, more for cake tin	6 oz
2.5 ml	salt	½ tsp
5 ml	baking powder	1 tsp
1	lemon	1
625 g	apples	1¼ lb
60 g	unsalted butter, more for cake tin	2 oz
200 g	sugar	6½ oz
2	eggs	2
60 ml	milk	4 tbsp
	For the glaze	
60 ml	water	4 tbsp
60 g	sugar	2 oz

ORDER OF WORK

1 MAKE THE CAKE
　 BATTER

2 BAKE THE CAKE
　 AND MAKE THE
　 GLAZE

MAKE THE CAKE BATTER

Vegetable peeler removes apple peel easily

1 Heat the oven to 180°C (350°F, Gas 4). Brush the springform tin with melted butter and sprinkle with a little flour, discarding the excess. Sift the measured flour with the salt and baking powder. Grate the zest from the lemon.

2 Peel the apples with the vegetable peeler. Cut the lemon in half and rub the cut surface of the lemon over the apples so they do not discolour.

3 With the point of the small knife, cut around the stalk end of each apple, and remove the stalk. Repeat with the flower end.

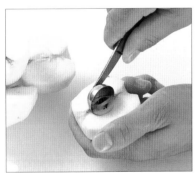

Slice apples very thinly so they cook quickly

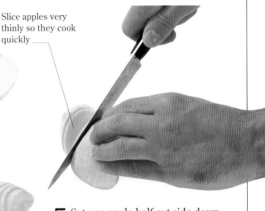

4 Cut the apples lengthwise in half. With the melon baller, carefully scoop out the core and seeds from the centre of each apple half, leaving as neat a shape as possible.

5 Set one apple half cut-side down. Cut the apple across into thin slices. Repeat for the other apple halves. Squeeze the remaining juice from the lemon halves over the apple slices.

6 Using the electric mixer, beat the butter in a large bowl until soft and creamy. Add the sugar and grated lemon zest and continue beating until light and crumbly, 2–3 minutes.

7 Add the eggs one by one to the creamed butter and sugar mixture, beating well after each addition.

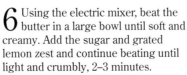

9 Sift in the flour mixture and stir gently with the rubber spatula until evenly mixed. Stir in half of the apple slices.

8 Gradually beat in the milk, and continue beating until the batter is very smooth.

Mix in flour gently with rubber spatula

2 BAKE THE CAKE AND MAKE THE GLAZE

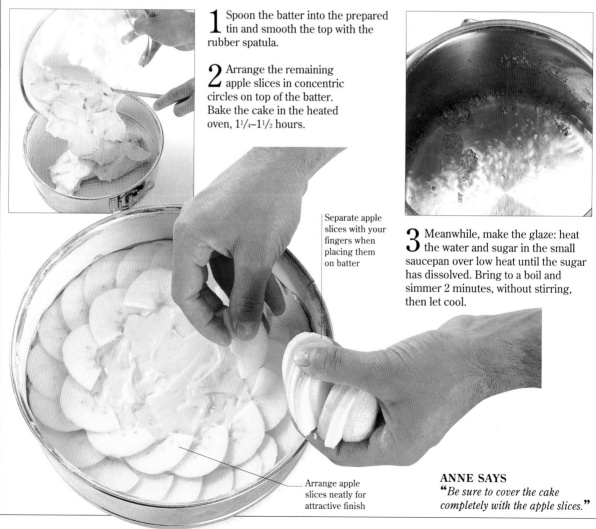

1 Spoon the batter into the prepared tin and smooth the top with the rubber spatula.

2 Arrange the remaining apple slices in concentric circles on top of the batter. Bake the cake in the heated oven, $1^1/_4$–$1^1/_2$ hours.

Separate apple slices with your fingers when placing them on batter

3 Meanwhile, make the glaze: heat the water and sugar in the small saucepan over low heat until the sugar has dissolved. Bring to a boil and simmer 2 minutes, without stirring, then let cool.

Arrange apple slices neatly for attractive finish

ANNE SAYS
"Be sure to cover the cake completely with the apple slices."

4 The cake is done when it shrinks slightly from the side of the tin and the skewer inserted in the centre comes out clean.

Brush glaze over apples while they are hot

5 Brush the sugar syrup glaze on top of the cake as soon as it comes out of the oven. Let the cake cool in the tin.

ANNE SAYS
"The cake will still be moist after it has been baked."

🍴 TO SERVE
Remove the side of the tin, then transfer the cake to a serving plate.

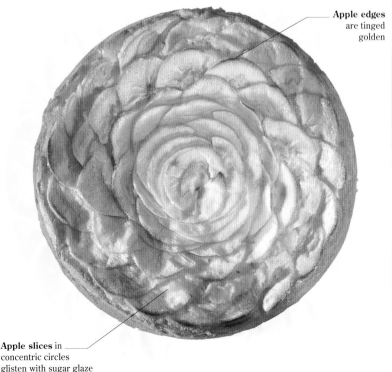

Apple edges are tinged golden

Apple slices in concentric circles glisten with sugar glaze

V A R I A T I O N

PEAR CAKE

Sautéed pears take the place of apples to make this Torta di Pere. *Use firm pears such as Conference.*

1 Butter and flour a 23 cm (9 inch) square cake tin, as directed.
2 Omit the apples and grated lemon zest. Peel and core 1 kg (2 lb) pears. Cut each pear half into 4 wedges and sprinkle with lemon juice.
3 Heat 30 g (1 oz) butter in a large frying or sauté pan, add the pears and sprinkle with 45–60 g (1¹/₂–2 oz) sugar. Sauté the pears, turning them once or twice, until golden, 7–10 minutes.
4 Remove the pears with a slotted spoon. Reserve 3–4 wedges. Cut the remaining wedges in 2–3 pieces and let them cool slightly.
5 Prepare the batter as directed, adding 5 ml (1 tsp) vanilla essence to the butter and sugar. Add the pear pieces to the batter and spoon it into the cake tin.
6 Arrange the remaining pear wedges on the surface of the batter in a decorative pattern (they will sink into the batter during baking).
7 Bake the cake as directed, 45 minutes only. Omit the sugar syrup glaze.
8 Let the cake cool in the tin, then turn it out onto a piece of aluminium foil and immediately flip the cake onto a serving board.
9 Cut into triangular wedges to serve.

ANNE SAYS
"If you have some syrup left when you have drained the pears it will make a delicious glaze for the baked cake."

WHIPPED CREAM CAKE WITH CHOCOLATE AND NUTS

Zuccotto Toscano

🍽 SERVES 8   🥣 WORK TIME 45–50 MINUTES*   ♨ BAKING TIME 25–30 MINUTES

EQUIPMENT

electric mixer†

baking sheet

bowls

chef's knife

pastry brush

kitchen scissors

vegetable peeler

thick cardboard

palette knife

2 wide spatulas

wire rack

greaseproof paper

rubber spatula

serrated knife

saucepans

cling film

20 cm (8 inch) square cake tin   sieves

† whisk can also be used

The name zuccotto *derives from* zucca, *meaning pumpkin, a reference to the hemispherical shape of this Florentine speciality, made of sponge cake, cream, and chocolate. You can save time by using 500 g (1 lb) of bought cake.*

*plus at least 6 hours chilling time

metric	SHOPPING LIST	imperial
	For the sponge cake	
60 g	unsalted butter, more for cake tin	2 oz
125 g	plain flour, more for cake tin	4 oz
	salt	
4	eggs	4
135 g	granulated sugar	4 ¹/₂ oz
	oil for bowl	
75 ml	Grand Marnier	2¹/₂ fl oz
	For the chocolate and nut filling	
90 g	slivered almonds	3 oz
175 g	plain chocolate	6 oz
500 ml	double cream	16 fl oz
60 g	icing sugar	2 oz
	For the decoration	
15 g	cocoa powder	¹/₂ oz
10 ml	icing sugar	2 tsp
1	bar of plain chocolate	1

INGREDIENTS

Grand Marnier†

double cream

plain chocolate

chocolate bar

icing sugar

unsalted butter

granulated sugar

plain flour

eggs

slivered almonds   cocoa powder

†any other orange-flavoured liqueur can also be used

ORDER OF WORK

1 MAKE THE SPONGE CAKE

2 PREPARE THE CHOCOLATE AND NUT FILLING

3 ASSEMBLE THE CAKE

4 UNMOULD AND DECORATE THE CAKE

1 MAKE THE SPONGE CAKE

1 Heat the oven to 180°C (350°F, Gas 4). Brush the cake tin with melted butter. Line the bottom with a square of greaseproof paper. Brush the paper with butter, sprinkle the tin with flour, and discard the excess flour.

2 Melt the butter in a small saucepan, and let cool. Meanwhile, sift the flour and a pinch of salt into a bowl.

4 Beat at high speed until the mixture leaves a ribbon trail when the beaters are lifted, 3–5 minutes.

ANNE SAYS
"If using a hand whisk, set the bowl over a saucepan of hot, but not boiling, water and whisk vigorously, about 10 minutes."

3 Put the eggs in a large bowl and beat a few seconds just to mix. Beat in the granulated sugar, using the electric mixer.

5 Sift about one-third of the flour mixture over the egg mixture and fold them together as lightly as possible. Add the remaining flour in the same way in 2 batches.

7 Pour the batter into the prepared cake tin and gently tap the tin on the work surface to level the batter and knock out any air bubbles. Bake at once, near the bottom of the heated oven, until the cake has risen and is firm to the touch when lightly pressed with a fingertip, 25–30 minutes. Remove the cake tin from the oven and leave the oven on.

Transfer cake to rack so steam can escape

6 Just after folding in the last batch of flour, add the cooled, melted butter and fold it in gently but quickly with the rubber spatula.

8 Turn the cake onto the wire rack and peel off the paper. Let the cake cool. Meanwhile, prepare the chocolate and nut filling (see page 118).

2 · PREPARE THE CHOCOLATE AND NUT FILLING

2 With the chef's knife, finely chop the chocolate. Alternatively, chop the chocolate in a food processor, using the pulse button.

ANNE SAYS
"On a warm day, chill chocolate before you chop it."

Use broad end of knife to chop chocolate, holding tip with other hand

1 Spread the almonds on the baking sheet and bake in the heated oven until lightly browned, stirring often so that they colour evenly, 8–10 minutes. Do not let them burn or they will be bitter. Let cool completely.

HOW TO WHIP AND SWEETEN CREAM

Double cream, with a minimum of 48% butterfat content, is best for whipping, and it should be thoroughly chilled in the refrigerator beforehand. Whipped cream can be covered and refrigerated up to 4 hours. It may separate slightly but will thicken again if whipped briefly.

1 Pour the double cream into a chilled medium-sized bowl placed in a larger bowl of iced water.

2 With an electric mixer or whisk, whip until the cream forms soft peaks.

4 For stiff peaks, continue whipping until the blades of the mixer or whisk leave clear marks in the cream.

! TAKE CARE !
If overwhipped, the cream will separate and turn to butter. When this is about to happen, it looks granular.

3 Add the sugar and whip until the cream forms soft peaks again and just holds its shape.

3 Whip the cream with the icing sugar until stiff peaks form (see box, page 118). Fold the toasted almonds with half of the chocolate into the whipped cream. Cover the mixture and chill.

4 Heat the remaining chocolate in a bowl set in a saucepan of hot water, stirring occasionally, just until melted. Leave until cool, but do not let it harden.

ASSEMBLE THE CAKE

1 Using the serrated knife, cut the cake into 3 equal triangles. Reserve the 2 small triangles from the sides. Cut each of the large triangles horizontally into 3 layers, to give 9 layers in all.

Slice large triangles of cake to make 9 equal pieces

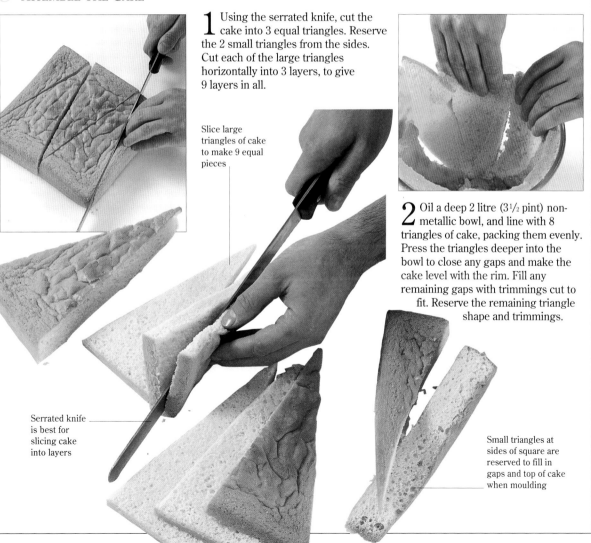

2 Oil a deep 2 litre (3½ pint) non-metallic bowl, and line with 8 triangles of cake, packing them evenly. Press the triangles deeper into the bowl to close any gaps and make the cake level with the rim. Fill any remaining gaps with trimmings cut to fit. Reserve the remaining triangle shape and trimmings.

Serrated knife is best for slicing cake into layers

Small triangles at sides of square are reserved to fill in gaps and top of cake when moulding

3 If necessary, trim the top edge of the cake even with the rim of the bowl. Brush the cake lining with the Grand Marnier.

4 Spoon half of the whipped cream filling into the cake-lined bowl. With the spoon, spread the filling evenly up the side of the cake lining, leaving a hollow in the middle. Chill in the refrigerator while you prepare the remaining filling.

Use rubber spatula to scrape every last bit of mixture from bowl

5 Add the cooled melted chocolate to the remaining whipped cream and fold until combined.

! TAKE CARE !
If the chocolate is still warm it will melt the cream.

6 Fill the hollow in the middle of the cake with the chocolate cream, smoothing the top with the rubber spatula.

7 Arrange the reserved large triangle over the filling. Cut the reserved small triangles horizontally in half and use to cover the filling completely, together with the reserved trimmings.

8 Cut a round of cardboard slightly smaller than the diameter of the bowl. Set on top of the cake, cover with cling film, and set a 500 g (1 lb) weight on top. Refrigerate until set, at least 6 hours.

4 UNMOULD AND DECORATE THE CAKE

1 Remove the weight and cling film. Run the palette knife around the edge of the zuccotto, easing it away from the bowl. Set a board on top of the bowl and invert them. Lift off the bowl.

2 Put the cocoa powder in a small sieve and sprinkle it generously over the zuccotto to cover the cake.

3 Put the icing sugar in the sieve and sprinkle it lightly over the top of the zuccotto. Using the vegetable peeler, shave curls from the bar of chocolate. Spoon the curls onto the centre of the zuccotto. Using 2 wide spatulas, transfer the cake, with the cardboard round, to a serving plate.

Dusting of cocoa powder and icing sugar gives cake neat finish

Chocolate curls are a simple but effective garnish

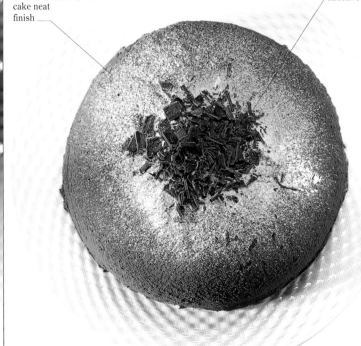

V A R I A T I O N

MOCHA WHIPPED CREAM CAKE
Mocha-flavoured whipped cream and Amaretti biscuits fill this Torta Moka.

1 Make the sponge cake as directed in the main recipe. If necessary, trim any crusty edges from the cake.
2 Using a long serrated knife, cut the cake horizontally into 3 even layers.
3 Brush the cake with Amaretto liqueur instead of Grand Marnier.
4 Omit the almonds and plain chocolate. Roughly chop 30 (about 150 g/5 oz) Amaretti biscuits.
5 Whip the cream as directed, adding 45 ml (3 tbsp) cocoa powder and 15 ml (1 tbsp) instant coffee powder with the icing sugar. Fold in one-third of the chopped Amaretti biscuits.
6 Spread a little of the mocha whipped cream mixture on the bottom layer of the cake, top with the middle cake layer, and spread with a little more whipped cream mixture.
7 Cover with the top cake layer and spread the remaining mocha mixture over the top and sides so they are covered. Press the remaining chopped biscuits onto the sides. Cut into 8 slices to serve.

GETTING AHEAD
The cake can be made up to 1 day ahead and kept in its covered bowl in the refrigerator. Unmould and decorate no more than 2 hours before serving; keep in a cool place.

ITALIAN KNOW-HOW

EQUIPMENT

A minimum of equipment is required for preparing an Italian meal. First priority is a good set of sharp knives. In a traditional Italian kitchen you won't find a food processor, but in some of the recipes in this book it will save you time chopping and puréeing. A blender can usually be used instead of a food processor, but the ingredients may need to be worked in batches. For cooking pasta, a pan large enough to hold at least 4 litres (7 pints) of water is essential. Heavy casseroles with lids are indispensable when braising meats such as pork, lamb, and beef on top of the stove or in the oven – use a pan with a thick base to prevent scorching during long, slow cooking.

If you have a pasta machine, now is the time to use it, although with patience you can roll your own pasta by hand. Baking dishes of various shapes and sizes come in handy when preparing many of these recipes. I like to use an attractive baking dish that can be transferred from oven to table, so the food can be served piping hot directly from the dish. Other standard kitchen equipment includes a vegetable peeler, grater, and lemon squeezer, as well as wooden spoons for stirring, and slotted spoons for lifting foods out of liquid or fat. You will need a frying pan and a colander or large sieve. A baking sheet is necessary for toasting nuts and for baking biscuits. Certain desserts call for a springform tin with a removable side – an easy way to unmould delicate cakes.

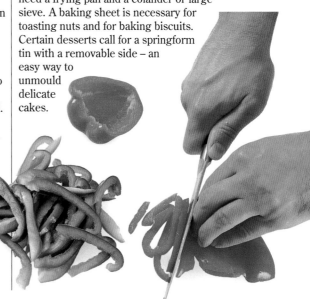

BEEF OR VEAL STOCK

Beef or veal stock is based on raw meat bones that are gently simmered with aromatic vegetables in water. Ask your butcher to cut the bones into pieces. Boiling should be avoided because it makes the stock cloudy.

🍽 MAKES 2–3 LITRES (3½–5 PINTS)

🥄 WORK TIME 20–30 MINUTES

🍲 COOKING TIME 4–5 HOURS

SHOPPING LIST

2 kg	beef or veal bones, cut in pieces	4½ lb
2	onions	2
2	carrots	2
2	celery sticks	2
4 litres	water, more if needed	7 pints
1	large bouquet garni	1
10	black peppercorns	10
1	garlic clove	1
15 ml	tomato purée	1 tbsp

1 Heat the oven to 230°C (450°F, Gas 8). Put the bones in a large roasting tin and roast until they are well browned, 30–40 minutes, stirring occasionally. Peel and quarter the onions and carrots. Quarter the celery. Add the vegetables to the tin and roast until brown, 15–20 minutes.

2 With a slotted spoon, transfer the bones and vegetables to a stockpot. Discard the fat from the roasting tin and add 500 ml (16 fl oz) of the water. Bring to a boil, stirring to dissolve the juices.

3 Add the liquid to the stockpot with all the remaining ingredients, then add enough water just to cover the bones. Bring slowly to a boil, skimming often with a large metal spoon. As soon as the liquid comes to a boil, lower the heat, and simmer very gently, uncovered, 4–5 hours, skimming occasionally. Add more water, if needed, to keep the bones covered.

4 Strain the stock, then taste it. If the flavour is not strong enough, boil the stock to reduce until concentrated. Let the stock cool, then chill in the refrigerator. When cold, the fat on the surface will be solid and easy to discard.

CHICKEN STOCK

Chicken stock is an indispensable ingredient in many recipes. Salt and pepper are not added to stock, because it is often reduced in individual recipes to concentrate the flavour. It keeps well up to 3 days, covered, in the refrigerator, or it can be frozen.

🍴 MAKES ABOUT 2 LITRES (3¼ PINTS)

🥣 WORK TIME 15 MINUTES

🍲 COOKING TIME UP TO 3 HOURS

SHOPPING LIST

1 kg	raw chicken backs and necks	2–2½ lb
1	onion	1
1	carrot	1
1	celery stick	1
1	bouquet garni	1
5	peppercorns	5
2 litres	water, more if needed	3¼ pints

1 Put the chicken in a large saucepan. Quarter the onion, carrot, and celery stick and add to the pan with the bouquet garni and peppercorns.

2 Add water just to cover the ingredients. Bring to a boil and simmer up to 3 hours, skimming occasionally with a large metal spoon. Add more water if necessary to keep the ingredients covered.

ANNE SAYS
"The longer the chicken stock is simmered, the more flavour it will have."

3 Strain the stock into a large bowl. Cool, then cover, and keep in the refrigerator.

ANNE SAYS
"If you do not make stock at home, buy a good consommé or use stock cubes."

FISH STOCK

Bones, including the heads and tails, of lean white fish, especially flatfish such as sole, are recommended for fish stock. Avoid oily fish such as mackerel. Fish stock keeps up to 2 days, covered, in the refrigerator, or it can be frozen.

🍴 MAKES ABOUT 1 LITRE (1⅔ PINTS)

🥣 WORK TIME 10–15 MINUTES

🍲 COOKING TIME 20 MINUTES

SHOPPING LIST

500 g	fish bones	1 lb
1	onion	1
250 ml	white wine or juice of ½ lemon	8 fl oz
1 litre	water	1⅔ pints
3–5	sprigs of parsley	3–5
5 ml	peppercorns	1 tsp

1 Thoroughly wash the fish bones. Cut the bones into 4–5 pieces with a chef's knife. Peel the onion, leaving a little of the root attached, then cut it lengthwise in half. Lay each onion half flat on a chopping board and cut across into thin slices.

2 Put the fish bones in a medium saucepan with the onion slices, white wine or lemon juice, water, parsley sprigs, and peppercorns. Bring to a boil and simmer 20 minutes. Skim the stock occasionally with a large metal spoon.

! TAKE CARE !
Do not simmer the fish stock too long or it will have a bitter taste.

3 Strain the stock into a bowl. Let cool, then cover and keep in the refrigerator.

ANNE SAYS
"I never season stock with salt and ground pepper at the time of making, because it might need to be reduced later in individual recipes, and the flavours will intensify."

INGREDIENTS

Fresh ingredients, particularly vegetables, are the backbone of meals in the Italian countryside. Aubergines, peppers, courgettes, artichokes, escarole, and, of course, tomatoes spring at once to mind as typically Italian, but don't forget spinach, carrots, peas, celery, and potatoes as well. They all appear with pasta, braised with meats, as main courses, and as side dishes. Always choose the freshest vegetables, and buy only those you need so they do not spoil in your refrigerator.

Olive oil is a mainstay – the highest quality unrefined and cold-pressed is at its best added uncooked to dishes such as salads or pasta just before serving. Indeed, on many family tables, a bottle of hearty, cold-pressed olive oil appears as a condiment, much as other countries use salt and pepper. Refined olive oils are less fruity and are lighter in both colour and flavour. They are best for sautéing and frying, or in recipes where the olive flavour is not important. Not surprisingly, in light of the climate, a wide array of aromatic herbs such as basil, oregano, flat-leaf parsley, mint, thyme, rosemary, and sage frequently find their way into Italian dishes. Whether they are stirred in at the last minute to donate fresh flavour and colour, or added at the beginning of cooking so they blend with other ingredients, herbs are an integral part of Italian cuisine. Equally important is the allium family – onion, garlic, leek, and shallot – while piquant flavourings such as dried chillies, olives, capers, anchovies, vinegar, and lemon juice add a further dimension.

Many Italian recipes are based on cereals and grains. Arborio rice, thicker and shorter than the more familiar long-grain, is best for risotto. Cornmeal (for polenta) and wheat flour are mandatory in any Italian kitchen. Fish, poultry, or meat is usually served as the *secondo piatto*. Flavours are often intensified by the addition of stock or wine. Chicken, beef, and fish stocks add background flavour to dishes, but if the recipe requires slow cooking and strong-flavoured ingredients, water can usually be substituted for stock with little loss of flavour. Marsala, Amaretto, and grappa are also called for in this book.

Cheeses play a significant role in Italian cooking, acting as a main ingredient in cakes, a binder for stuffings, toppings for browning, or simply adding flavour to a dish. Freshly grated Parmesan, semi-soft fontina, blue-veined Gorgonzola, fresh ricotta, and mozzarella are frequently used in the recipes that I have chosen.

When it comes to Italian country desserts, fruits such as apples, pears, strawberries, and raspberries provide natural sweetness, while chocolate, coffee, caramel, and nuts lend their characteristic tastes to cakes and biscuits.

ITALIAN COUNTRY COOKING AND YOUR HEALTH

If you are especially concerned about fat content and calories, here are some points to consider when preparing Italian food. Olive oil, a fundamental ingredient in Italian cooking, is high in mono-unsaturated fat and has no cholesterol at all. You are therefore already taking a step in the right direction towards a healthier diet by choosing **Italian Country Cooking**. In addition, grains and vegetables are always present. Whether they are in a simple green salad and a piece of crusty bread or combined, as in Fresh Polenta with Vegetable Stew, they serve to balance the Italian menu. To lower your overall fat intake, look first of all for recipes that rely on ingredients that are naturally low in fat, such as Grilled Mussels with Red Pepper Topping, and Devilled Chicken. If your concern is cholesterol, turn to dishes in which saturated fat can easily be eliminated or replaced. For instance, use olive oil instead of butter when making Asparagus Risotto and when tossing pasta.

The richness of other recipes can be reduced by leaving out certain ingredients. Omit the meatballs in Baked Rigatoni and the bacon in Quills with Spicy Tomato and Bacon Sauce. Spinach and Potato Gnocchi lend themselves to any sauce, so substitute a favourite vegetable topping for the Tomato-Cream Sauce.

Though rich desserts are hard to resist, large quantities of cream and butter add up to high calories. Choose Grapefruit or Coffee Granita and reduce the sugar, or omit it completely. Use low-fat ricotta cheese in the Ricotta Cheesecake, omit the almonds, and serve thinner slices to satisfy any sweet tooth.

MICROWAVE

Many of these Italian recipes can be adapted for microwave cooking, to speed preparation. Roman-Style Artichokes, for instance, can be cooked in the microwave. Cooking time for Braised Pork with Madeira Sauce can be cut significantly by roasting the meat, tightly covered, in the microwave, then finishing it in a hot oven for a crispy exterior. The lengthy cooking for Beef Braised in Red Wine can also be reduced: brown the beef on top of the stove, then simmer it in the microwave. However, be careful not to add too much liquid and not to cook the beef too long or it will be stringy. You can also save time in other recipes by using the microwave for steaming clams in Grilled Clams, and blanching spinach for Spinach and Potato Gnocchi in Tomato-Cream Sauce and Spinach-Stuffed Veal Rolls (spinach retains its bright green colour when cooked in the microwave).

Don't forget that some basic preparations are easy in the microwave. You can peel onions, garlic, and tomatoes: heat onions and garlic cloves at High (100 % power), 45–50 seconds for onions, 15–30 seconds for garlic; put tomatoes in boiling water in a microwave-safe bowl and cook until the skins split, 10–15 seconds. You can also cook bacon, melt chocolate, and even cook caramel in the microwave.

TECHNIQUES

A wide range of basic techniques is illustrated in these recipes, some specifically Italian but others of more general application. You can see how to make fresh pasta and potato gnocchi, and how to cook polenta. There are instructions on how to make a simple tomato sauce, as well as richer cream sauces, and how to clean and cook mussels and clams. To give extra flavour, olive oil, lemon juice, wine vinegar, and a

variety of herbs and spices are used to marinate some ingredients, either before or after cooking. Once mastered, these techniques can be applied to a number of different recipes in this book.

Cooking methods in this book are equally varied, ranging from sautéing chicken in the recipe for Hunter's Chicken to pan-frying fish in Sole Fillets Marinated in Wine Vinegar. Grilling, braising, roasting, and simmering are other important techniques that are covered.

As with other volumes in the *Look & Cook* series, basic techniques are described in detail: how to chop herbs; how to peel, seed, and chop tomatoes; how to chop and slice onions; how to roast, peel, and seed peppers; how to core, seed, and dice fresh chillies; how to make chicken, fish, and beef or veal stock – these are all fully explained.

The desserts cover important basics such as making pastry shells, baking sponge cakes, toasting nuts, whipping cream, and making caramel.

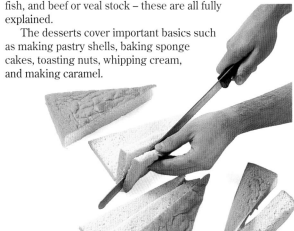

HOW-TO BOXES

In each of the recipes in **Italian Country Cooking** *you'll find pictures of all the techniques used. However, some basic preparations appear in a number of recipes, and they are shown in extra detail in these special "how-to" boxes:*

INDEX

ACKNOWLEDGEMENTS

Photographers David Murray
Juies Selmes
Photographer's Assistant Ian Boddy

Chef Eric Treuille
Cookery Consultants Martha Holmberg
Annie Nichols
Home Economist Sarah Lowman

Typesetting Linda Parker
Text film by Disc to Print (UK) Ltd

Production Consultant Lorraine Baird

*Carroll & Brown Limited
would like to thank ICTC
(0181 568-4179) for supplying the
Cuisinox Elysee pans used throughout the
book, The Kitchenware Merchants
Limited for the Le Creuset cookware, and
Magimix (UK) Limited who supplied the
Cuisine Systeme food processor.*

*Anne Willan owes special thanks to
consultant Henry Grossi for his
invaluable guidance on Italian recipes
and cooking techniques.*

*She would also like to thank her chief
editor Kate Krader and associate editors
Stacy Toporoff and Jacqueline Bobrow,
together with Cynthia Nims, for their
vital help with writing this book and
researching and testing the recipes,
aided by La Varenne's chefs and
trainees.*

NOTES

- Metric and imperial measures have been calculated separately. Only use one set of measures as they are not exact equivalents.

- All spoon measurements are level.

- Spoon measurements are calculated using a standard 5 ml teaspoon and 15 ml tablespoon to give an accurate measurement of small amounts.